W9-BHG-587

CHRISTIANITY, JUDAISM, AND REVOLUTION

CHRISTIANITY, JUDAISM,

AND

REVOLUTION

WILFRIED DAIM

Translated by PETER TIRNER

FREDERICK UNGAR PUBLISHING CO.

NEW YORK

Published by arrangement with Manz Verlag, Munich.

Copyright © 1973 by Frederick Ungar Publishing Co., Inc.
Printed in the United States of America
Library of Congress Catalog Card Number: 73-163148
Designed by Irving Perkins
ISBN: 0-8044-5266-0

CONTENTS

FOREWORD

This book was written in the years 1963 and 1964. But the experiences on which it rests are very much older. They began with the experience of an ever-questioning Roman Catholic upbringing whose highest ideal was "meekness," that is, obedience to any kind of authority.

When Hitler, a fellow Austrian, began to organize with utmost cynicism the most gigantic mass murder in all history, the vast majority of Austrian Catholics persisted in this "meekness" in which they had been brought up. The Christian thesis of the right to resistance—whose rudiments are present but play almost no role in practical catechetics—was not implemented in these circumstances. A genuine Christian doctrine of revolution was lacking.

Yet all of the great political powers in existence today stand on revolutionary foundations: the United States of America, the Soviet Union, China, and so on. The independence movements throughout the world that are shaking off colonialism are indications that new principles are coming to the fore.

For Christianity, it has become a matter of life and death to reach a thorough understanding of the revolutionary element in today's society, even if only for the purpose of gaining deeper insight into revolutionary aspirations so that they can be dealt with more successfully. Such understanding can best be achieved if we single out and face up to those elements in ourselves that are similar to, akin to, or identical with the elements of revolution.

We are thus confronted with the task of raising into the light of full awareness Christianity's basic revolutionary element, and thus to make it fruitful for our day. In making this attempt, I was aided by the persistent charge that such brilliant intellectual gadflies as Nietzsche, Evola, and Klages have cast at Christianity and Judaism: the charge that both these creeds had played a decisive role in every revolutionary movement (at least in recent centuries), as well as in the decay of the Roman Empire, and have indeed been at the root of every revolutionary upheaval.

Though I reject the evaluation that National Socialism placed on communism and liberalism, I am entirely convinced that all revolutionary movements in the old world and the new share a common Judeo-Christian root, and that liberalism, socialism, and communism flow from the same Judeo-Christian source. This I see, however, as a credit to Judaism and Christianity, not as a deplorable consequence of their teaching that would cast a shadow on their histories.

In venturing to approach the Bible with the insights of modern social psychology, we find ourselves coming closer to the archetypal revolutionary drive. We come to understand the Jewish archetypal revolution and the central role that Judaism has played in history. The history of the Jews —from Abraham to Simon Peter—is the backbone of world history. And this is the case, as I propose to show, not just in terms of religious history or the history of salvation, but, in the most concrete sense, in terms of political history as well.

If my book were to awaken within Christendom a deeper understanding of the Jewish roots of Christianity, if it were to constitute a step in the direction of identification of Christianity with Judaism, much would be gained. To me, it seems necessary that Christianity and Judaism pass through their present phase of coexistence and enter into communication. This communication is far more important than that between liberalism and Marxism or that between either of these and Christianity. Once Christianity understands its own Jewish roots, an understanding of revolutionary movements is no longer an intellectual problem or difficult to achieve. There is, of course, more to Judaism and to Christianity than is presented in this book; I merely hope for the increasing realization that those elements that I point out here are of basic importance. For in that case, there is the possibility that Christianity become reconciled with revolution—and revolution become reconciled with Christianity.

— WILFRIED DAIM

All quotations from the Bible are from the Authorized King James version.

INTRODUCTION

EVER SINCE THE MIDDLE AGES, Roman Catholic moral theology has occasionally dealt with man's right to resist the authority of princes and of any kind of illegitimate authority. Most recently, such a right was confirmed once more in John XXIII's encyclical Pacem in Terris:

> Therefore, when governmental authorities fail to recognize, or when they violate, the rights of man, they are not only neglectful of their duties, but their regulations lose all legal sanction.

For our present purposes, we need not enter upon the complexities arising from the fact that the precise nature of the rights of man is controversial. Besides, the formulation is couched in those general terms that are so typical of encyclicals. They barely hint at the subtly varied, complex, and portentous problems of every true revolution, problems that recur with considerable regularity.

A revolution is far more than mere resistance. The removal of a potentate who breaks the laws of the land, and his replacement by another, perhaps more conscientious ruler, may be a legal and just event, but it is not a genuine revolution. The objective of a genuine revolution is to lay a new foundation for society, to introduce a new principle of human community. It challenges the very basis of society, and provides the doctrines of natural law with a new content. The thesis "to each his own!" has a wholly different meaning for the aristocrat of the *ancien régime* and for the citizen of the French Revolution.

1

To the aristocrat, "to each his own!" signifies an affirmation of the "natural" privileges of noble birth. The "nature" of the man of aristocratic birth implies certain lordly rights; the "nature" of the peasant child, on the other hand, implies that he is at the bottom of society. But in natural law as conceived in bourgeois thought, man's "nature" has a totally different complexion. "To each his own!" implies no privileges of birth: Human equality begins to assume a genuine meaning.

By their revolution the French bourgeoisie intended to establish a new basis of society. Similarly, the instigators of the February revolution, and even more, of the November revolution in Russia in 1917 hoped to establish a new basis of society. To lay new foundations for society is something altogether different from mere resistance against arbitrary government. The replacement of an authority by one that will adhere more closely to the law, while still maintaining the same social system, is something altogether different from challenging the basis of the law itself.

This new principle of social structure, the initial revolt, the organization of the counterrevolution and the revolutionary counterthrust provoked by it, the phase of terror which then follows—these are among the elements that are typical of revolutions.

What I am attempting in this book is a return to the revolutionary roots of the Judeo-Christian religion. Now that Hitler's gas chambers have discredited antisemitism even within the church, there exists a much greater willingness within Christianity to acknowledge its own Judaic origins and consequently perhaps also that revolutionary power that radiates from Mount Sinai. For Christianity will ultimately have to come to terms with that power, although it may take many decades, because it offers the precious opportunity to gather into the fold the great revolutions of recent centuries, and to make peace with the American, the French, the Soviet, and the revolution of communist China.

One more remark, on my method: I rarely raise the question of the historical truth of biblical reports. The problems with which I am dealing are primarily socio-psychological rather than historical; and the political-psychological effects of a tale may be of equal strength, whether that tale is historical, or mythological, or a mixture of the two. Had Moses never existed, it would in no way diminish the profound effect he will exert in times to come, still less his effect in the past. Had he never existed, it would mean simply that the Jewish people, by creating the figure of Moses, have created the archetype of revolution. Whenever I have considered matters of historical authenticity, as I have on a few occasions, it seemed to be justified by the context.

I.

AFFIRMATION OF THE NEW
AUTHORITY: ABRAHAM

Either there is the paradox, that the individual
stands in an absolute relation to the absolute—or
Abraham is lost.

—Søren Kierkegaard

ALTHOUGH the two great landmarks of Christian existence
are linked to the two names, Jesus and Moses, yet there are
other figures of great importance that came before and
after and between these two. Perhaps the most important
figure before Moses is Abraham—Abraham with his crucial act, the sacrifice of Isaac. Søren Kierkegaard had every
reason to make this man and this act the central concern
of his meditations in his *Fear and Trembling*.

Let us, then, take a closer look at the background of
Abraham's action, and the heroic struggle in his heart:

Abraham hoped that his wife Sarah would bear him the
son promised him by an inner voice. Surely, his dialogue
with God must be interpreted as a dialogue with his own
conscience. It was the kind of experience that endows even
purely visionary insights with that absolute conviction that
is the mark of all true prophecy. Yet even this absolute
conviction, if it must be maintained over long stretches of
time, may be subject to moments of doubt. But Abraham

5

ultimately held fast to the vision of his faith: that he was destined to found a new generation, a new nation. Thus the founding of the Jewish nation begins with a highly improbable event and with a great sacrifice.

Then, after Sarah had indeed borne a son to Abraham in his old age, the child's survival hung in balance, just as later the survival of the Jewish nation was again and again to hang in balance.

Abraham named his son Isaac. He had him circumcised on the eighth day after birth, according to custom. And with that archaic, intuitive understanding of what are the most significant moments in the life of man, he gave a great feast on the day the boy was weaned. For on that day, the child was separated from his mother for a second time. And he was yet to separate himself from his father.

Let us imagine the relationship between the aged father and his son. Abraham no doubt "idolized" the boy. His attitude was bound to hamper Isaac's development profoundly, forcing him into his own way, and denying him the freedom that he needed to become authentically himself.

Thus there arose the fixations. In Abraham, the fixation upon an idol, the image of what his son should become. In Isaac, the fixation on the image that his father was imposing on him, which threatened to determine his entire future.

Deep in his heart Abraham must have felt that he was doing an injustice to Isaac—and to God as well, whose special claim on Isaac he wanted to deny. And from these roots sprang Abraham's intuitive conviction, which he understood as a divine call. "I must put my relation with God, with myself, and with Isaac in order."

At first, Abraham did not know clearly what needed to be done:

> Take now thy son, thine only *son* Isaac, whom thou
> lovest.
>
> (Genesis 22:2)

The Bible story emphasizes that Isaac is the only son, and that Abraham's love for him is exceedingly great. It goes on:

> offer him there for a burnt offering upon one of the
> mountains which I will tell thee of.
>
> (Genesis 22:2)

And Abraham is willing. Kierkegaard focused exclusively on the tremendous conflict within Abraham's breast. Kierkegaard sets this moral conflict at the very center of his thoughts, and uses the metaphor of weaning that leads us into the heart of depth psychology.

Abraham is directed to act in violation of every human law. He is to kill his son, to sacrifice him, defying his own fatherhood and his supreme love. His justification is that God commanded him to do so. There is, then, an authority above human authority; Abraham's relation to God is an immediate relation, it exists apart from all those other relations that lead to God through the mediation of other creatures. And this relation to the supreme authority reduces all human laws and rules to secondary importance.

If there were not this ultimate confrontation—if there were not, above human authority, another authority that can give man the right to break established law—then Abraham would have been a criminal. Thus Kierkegaard was able to say: "Either there is the paradox, that the individual stands in an absolute relation to the absolute— or Abraham is lost." Kierkegaard could call the "absolute relation to the absolute" a paradox, an absurdity, in the sense that its consequence could—as in Abraham's case— be an act running counter to the universal opinion of mankind. Without this absolute relation to God, Abraham would have to be condemned by this universal opinion, and therefore would be "lost."

The psychological problem with which Abraham here had to deal is worth our study: it is the problem of every sacrifice as such. Isaac was dearer to Abraham than anything else on earth. Was it sheer sadism that prompted God to ask for the sacrifice of the only son "whom you love"?

Kierkegaard delves into Abraham's state of mind, which the author of the Bible story ignores with stony detachment. God's terrible demand on Abraham to give up what is dearest to him in all the world, for God's sake, Abraham's despair and shock, his quarrel with God, his self-accusations—this is what Kierkegaard conjures up before us with penetrating power.

> When the child must be weaned, the mother blackens her breast, it would indeed be a shame that the breast should look delicious when the child must not have it. So the child believes that the breast has changed, but the mother is the same, her glance is as loving and tender as ever. Happy the person who had no need of more dreadful expedients for weaning the child!

Psychoanalytic investigations have shown that the experience of weaning is a grave event in every individual's development. But only in the last few decades has it been understood that the child when weaned is also being separated from an idol, from an individual's *summum bonum*. It is this separation process—the process by which the infant separates the mother from the mother's breast—that Kierkegaard compares with what went on in Abraham's soul. To Abraham the loveliness of the mother's breast is analogous to Isaac; the mother to God, who is as loving as ever.

This is the problem of individual maturity. Abraham has in a way abandoned his independence to Isaac. On certain levels of Abraham's soul—the emotional levels—Isaac had become Abraham's *summum bonum*. Because of this fact, Isaac stood in the way of Abraham's relation to God. He loomed too large, he was too much beloved, because Abraham made too much of him. Therefore Isaac had to be sacrificed. Here the meaning of the whole event stands revealed. Isaac had become an idol. Only Isaac's death could free Abraham from his fixation on Isaac and so reestablish his proper relation to a jealous God.

Because the purpose of the whole event is the education, the psychological development of Abraham, it is sufficient for the sacrifice to take place entirely in Abraham's mind. By following God's demand with absolute obedience, Abraham had in fact already made the sacrifice. He had bid his son "farewell" and had submitted to God's will. This is why Isaac was restored to him. But Isaac now no longer meant to him what he had meant before. Now their relation was less absolute, more distant. Once again, God was greater to Abraham than his son Isaac. Old as he was, Abraham grew by virtue of this renunciation: he was weaned and became more mature. It is in the maturing of Abraham that the meaning of the sacrifice lies. His relation to God has been rectified.

If, however, we regard Abraham's weaning as the sole purpose of the event, and Abraham as the sole object of the divine lesson, we would be making a mistake:

We would be overlooking the psychology of the victim, Isaac. True, Isaac's role is passive—but Abraham's action is of greater consequence for him than for Abraham himself, and of greater consequence also for the future history of Israel. What Isaac experiences is the profound transformation of an authority that having once confronted him as an absolute authority, now confronted him as a relative authority.

Kierkegaard, though only in passing, paid attention to the events in Isaac's mind. He described Isaac's reaction with poetic intuition:

> When Isaac again saw Abraham's face it was changed, his glance was wild, his form was horror . . . Then Isaac trembled and cried out in his terror, "O God in heaven, have compassion upon me. If I have no father upon earth, be Thou my father!"

The passage suggests that Isaac was being weaned from fatherly authority. To find a father, he now turned to God. The Bible mentions none of this, although it indicates that Abraham, up until the last moment, did not have the courage to open his heart to Isaac. But it cannot surprise us that the son turned to God when his own father was ready to kill him. Isaac's shock must have been all the more profound because he knew how much his father loved him.

But it was not this one traumatic experience alone that changed Isaac's view of Abraham, and made him see Abraham as less absolute than God. Isaac could not fail to notice that Abraham's attitude toward him had permanently changed. Abraham's renunciation of total control over Isaac, his sacrifice, his offering of Isaac to God, were bound to leave a lasting mark on Isaac's mind. Henceforth there would be a greater distance between father and son, which would make it possible for Abraham to give to Isaac the freedom that every person must have to achieve individual and full maturity.

To summarize, Abraham reduced his own authority by making it subordinate to that of God's. Henceforth Isaac had two fathers, one absolute, the other only relative. Isaac now stood in an absolute relation to the absolute.

What is the true meaning of this important archetypal event? According to Freud's speculations about the development of patriarchal authority, the sons in the primal horde probably killed the fathers until the deterrent of circular guilt developed. The killing of the father is provoked when the father is unwilling to allow autonomy to the son. (For a discussion of this pattern in revolutionary terms, see the appendix.) In contrast to the Freudian construction of patricide as a common pattern, the case of Abraham is an example of a filicide—though the killing is committed only on a psychological level. Abraham kills his own absolute authority over his son by giving him to God. By this event, the concept of the son's obligation to exercise total obedience toward the father underwent a radical transformation. Obedience to God is indisputably right; obedience to men is indisputably dubious. Abraham set Isaac free for God. By doing so, he limited Isaac's duty to be obedient to him. God's will was to be binding to Isaac just as he, Abraham, stood ready to break the law against killing when God called him to do so.

Is not this act of Abraham's the foundation of Moses's power later on to make his revolution? Is not this also the foundation upon which Jesus, invoking God's will when he did so, broke the law when quintessential matters were at stake? No doubt. And the same goes for Peter, who twice made bold to tell the high council,

> We ought to obey God rather than men.
> (Acts 5:29)

Thus he invoked man's conscience that had been sharpened by Abraham, Moses, and the prophets.

The high council did not know if it was God who spoke through Peter. It showed tolerance to Peter—as it did not do to Jesus—and abstained from claiming its authority to be absolute. It refrained from deciding whether it was dealing with wheat or with chaff. It followed Gamaliel's advice:

> Refrain from these men, and let them alone; for if this counsel or this work be of men, it will come to nought:
> But if it be of God, ye cannot overthrow it; lest haply ye be found even to fight against God.
> (Acts 5:38–39)

To "obey God rather than men"—this is the foundation of every revolution the thrust of which is in the direction of the evolution of mankind.

II.

THE GOD OF THE BURNING
THORNBUSH: MOSES

I AM THAT I AM: . . . I am the Lord thy God,
which have brought thee out of the land of Egypt,
out of the house of bondage.
> —God, according to the Book of Exodus
> (3:14; 20:2)

ABRAHAM'S SACRIFICE was no doubt basic in that it established a new relation between human and divine authority,
and provided the archetype that prepared Moses and the
Jews of Egypt to accomplish one of the mightiest deeds in
all history. Still, it was no more than a preparation. The
great deed—the founding of an egalitarian society, though
only in its rudimentary form—was left for another to perform.

Spiritual interpretations of the Bible, antisemitism
within and without the church, and a romanticized view
of classical antiquity have prevented us from coming to
the full awareness of the tremendous significance of Moses
in the history of revolution.

Still, the significance of Moses's action has been recognized by thinkers again and again. Adam Müller, in *Ele-
mente der Staatskunst* (Elements of Statecraft), published
in 1822, said of Moses: "The fashionable enthusiasm of our

age for Greek and Roman antiquity has crowded this great law-giver from the memory of the educated."

He also wrote: " . . . what pygmies are Leonidas and his Spartans, and all the Brutuses of history, compared with this gigantic hero of freedom."

If Christianity is now preparing, not just to make its peace with the great revolutions, but to take them to its bosom, then it is indeed high time for us to come to a full understanding of the figure of Moses.

But to understand Moses, his purpose, and his people, we must recall the situation in which he found himself.

1. *The Initial Situation*

The Jews of Egypt, once nomads, settled in Egypt more or less voluntarily, but eventually became enslaved. They seem to have inhabited a relatively contiguous area. The social gulf between them and the Egyptians must have been very wide. Egyptian society itself was a society of slaveholders, with a strictly hierarchical structure. It may be symbolized by a double pyramid, half visible, half invisible, the points of which are joined like the two glass bulbs of an hourglass.

At the apex of the visible pyramid (the lower one) was the pharaoh, master of the world. This society was as class conscious as aristocracies are wont to be. Indeed, there were periods when the pharaoh considered nobody his equal except his sisters. This can be seen as the origin of incestuous marriages in the Egyptian royal family.

The other pyramid, invisible, imaginary, is inverted: this was the hierarchy of the gods. The pharaoh was the highest among men—and the lowest among gods.

In that hierarchy, the Jews were lower even than the

Egyptians at the visible pyramid's base. Yet the Jews had a social structure of their own.

The Bible tells us that the Egyptians created a privileged class among the Jews. This class, in return for certain material advantages, served the Egyptians as their guards and supervisors, much as the kapos did in the Nazi concentration camps. It would indeed be strange if the intelligent Egyptians had not hit upon a method that has been practiced by the officers of every army throughout history. The dirty work, the torture of subjecting raw recruits to basic training, is left to corporals and sergeants. In the midst of the sadistic training, an officer might happen to come by and demonstrate his generosity by ordering the sergeant to ease up. The officer thus appears as the lesser evil. He has the greater power, and gains still greater respect by the technique just described, one that deflects the men's aggression and contempt on to their immediate superiors.

Even though generally the situation of the Jews was not like that of the Jews in a concentration camp, there was one command that the Bible tells us of, that could have been issued by the Nazis. A pharaoh—whose reign apparently was relatively short—commanded Jewish midwives to kill all Jewish male infants. His purpose may have been to eliminate potential insurgents. Jewish female infants were to be allowed to live, so that they would grow up to staff Egyptian harems, brothels, and to work as servants. The Jewish midwives, however, failed to obey. The pharaoh, thereupon, charged Egyptians to carry out the order.

A Levite woman bore a son. For a time she concealed him, but did not dare to continue to do so. To give him a chance to survive, she made a basket of papyrus rushes, placed the infant inside, and then abandoned him.

It might be objected that this abandonment, and even more so the threat to the infant's life by an evil authority, are echoes of the legends based on the archetypal heroes, and consequently indicate myth, not historical truth. Many a heroic myth tells of the evil father, or of an evil father surrogate, who orders his infant killed. The myth of Zeus is an example. Cronus commanded his wife to surrender all her children to him so that he may devour them. But she concealed her son Zeus, and in his stead fed Cronus a stone wrapped in swaddling clothes. Zeus grew up without his father knowing that he was still alive. Later, he revolted and overthrew his father.

This threat to life at the hour of birth is found in the biblical account of the life of Moses—and of the life of Christ. Moses is threatened by the pharaoh's ruling, Christ by Herod's decree. The pharaoh and Herod are the "evil fathers." In each case, a woman becomes the protector of the threatened infant.

But the similarity in detail between the myth and the Bible stories cannot be regarded as proof that the biblical accounts are not historical. We cannot brand every putative historical event as a fabrication simply because it exhibits certain similarities to a myth. The relations between myth and history are these:

(1) A historical fact is turned into an archetypal event by psychological reduction, and thus becomes a myth.

(2) A historical fact is altered—embroidered or the like —and thus becomes subsumed into a mythological schema (this would be a special case of item 1).

(3) A myth exists, and to conform to it, the people involved in a concrete situation adapt their actions accordingly.

(4) A myth expresses a psychological law. Therefore a historical process acts out law.

- 3 -

In actuality several of these aspects may be present, and may reinforce one another.

The rebellious child is more likely to grow up into a revolutionist if from his childhood he is confronted by an authority that impresses him as hostile. Martin Luther, who defied the pope himself, was the result of his relationship with an overbearing father. The mythological hero is symbolically expressive of the fact that a man who has been persecuted from childhood by an evil authority seems more predisposed to want to change society than one who has not had this experience. But this means only that myths are expressions of basic truths. The factual truth of a historic event is not invalidated because it exhibits certain parallels to the elements of myths.

Finally, we must recall the all-important fact that as long as a story reaching back to a nation's dawn is accepted by the nation as historic truth, it makes little difference to its socio-psychological effectiveness whether it is a myth or not.

That Moses's life was from its beginning threatened by the pharaohs serves to prove that he was genuinely predisposed to become a revolutionist. That evil authority did indeed almost succeed in killing Moses. It is typical of revolutionists to have survived by the skin of their teeth. Such survival leads one to believe in divine providence, if one is religious, or in a secularized view of historical determinism, if one is not.

The conduct of Moses's mother is altogether consistent with what most mothers would have done. The pharaoh's daughter, who rescued the abandoned infant, also behaved quite naturally. The assertion that Moses was "obviously" not a Jewish child, that he must have been the illegitimate son of the Egyptian princess, is without basis in the biblical text, our only source. This claim is based on the assertion that the finding of the infant Moses by the pharaoh's daughter—of all people—is altogether too much of a coincidence.

But the arrival of the princess is not as much of a coincidence as might appear at first glance. The uppermost concern of Moses's mother was to do everything in her power to assure her child's survival. If she knew the place where the princess usually went to bathe, and perhaps also knew the time of day she usually bathed, the finding of the baby is no longer a coincidence because Moses's mother would naturally have left the child at that place, at that hour.

Moses's mother may have staked her hopes on the chance that a woman would take pity on an abandoned child. Unwed mothers leave their children on church steps with very similar expectations. And Moses's mother would have more reason to hope that the pharaoh's edict would be set away this one time if the baby was taken in by a princess rather than an Egyptian commoner.

It is always conceivable that the author of Exodus may have had an interest in making Moses out to be a Jew rather than an Egyptian. But that is not proof that he falsified history. Besides, Moses's psychological development is explained much more readily if we follow the Bible story, rather than Freud whose study on Moses turns Moses into an Egyptian.

The princess, then, assumed responsibility for the baby; she hired his true mother to be his nurse, while she herself became his foster mother.

Moses's upbringing at the Egyptian court, and the psychological situation in which he was placed there, are of the utmost significance for his intellectual development. We must try to visualize that situation clearly.

As the protégé of a princess, Moses surely received the

very best of Egyptian schooling. He was educated like the future rulers, and probably had the same tutors as the princes of the palace. Thus he came to know the uses, and the limitations, of power—something a revolutionist needs to know—and learned to discern the weak points in the power structure, the points at which a future attack might be successfully directed. He was then a de facto member of the country's ruling class, though he did not belong to it by birth, and was not prevented from acquiring an insight into the workings of royal power and rule. These circumstances may have complicated his psychological make-up by excluding him from any class.

For, though Moses was materially well cared for, thanks to the princess's patronage, the people at the court must have treated him as a man of a lower class. His high intelligence, probably superior to that of the Egyptian princes, did not secure for him a socially superior position. He still was an intruder from below, an interloper, a man who could never overcome the stigma of low birth, however capable he was.

We can well imagine what a tutor at the court would do to a pupil of low birth who showed himself more intelligent than the pharaoh's own sons. The superior intelligence in such a pupil would be tantamount to a violation of the feudal ideology concerning the eminent hereditary endowment of princes of the royal blood. Any tutor would be bound to falsify Moses's scholastic achievements.

Moses, then, is a hero shaped by his environment, one whose profile conforms to the traditional portrait of the revolutionist.

His realization that his worth would not be acknowledged, that he could never rise to a position in keeping with his ability; the slighting treatment he must have suffered—all this was bound to drive him into an aggressive attitude toward the ruling Egyptian class and to a closer identification with his own people.

Revolutionists who are themselves members of the upper classes often feel one with the lower classes. Marx and Engels were both members of the bourgeoisie who sided with the proletariat and made its aspirations to social ascent their own. Lenin, the son of a small landholder, identified with the proletariat. Mao Tse-tung's father was a farmer of substance and a rice merchant, who treated Mao with contempt and hostility, as if he were one of the servants. Thus Mao became the peasants' revolutionary leader. He opposed his father by setting himself into opposition to the whole class to which his father belonged. Such revolutionists, when fighting for the equality of the underdog, are often fighting for their own equality. And they fight a social system in order to establish a new system, one that will not repeat the injustices of the old.

Clearly, his identification with his fellow Jews drove Moses, an outsider at the feudal court, to go out and observe the Jewish slaves at their labors. His solidarity with them must have been intense, his hatred of the Egyptians passionate. Thus, when he saw an Egyptian beating a Jew, he committed what can only be called a political murder. Nor was the deed committed in a fit of passion—it was a premeditated killing. The Bible is explicit:

> And he looked this way and that way, and when he saw that *there* was no man, he slew the Egyptian, and hid him in the sand.
>
> (Exodus 2:12)

This act committed by Moses raises many questions. But it is of extreme importance to our understanding of revolutionary ideologies. For as we study the Mosaic revolution, and compare it with the American, French, and Russian revolutions, we often encounter the defense that in Moses's case everything happened at God's command, while most other revolutionists were prompted by their own consciences.

The slaying of the Egyptian, however, is reported in the Bible without the least suggestion of a divine command. Divine command occurs only during Moses's experience at the burning thornbush. But it cannot be denied that the killing of the Egyptian is Moses's first active intervention on the part of the Jews, and that it belongs in the confines of the Mosaic revolution.

It is unlikely that the act contributed anything of value to the Mosaic revolution that lay ahead. Its immediate result was to draw the aggression of the pharaoh and his political police onto Moses. And it did nothing to help the Jews. The dead Egyptian was no doubt replaced at once by another, no friendlier than the first. Still, the experience was essential to Moses's own development. The killing was a blunder. Moses surely learned from this act of violence that, to effect a fundamental change, nothing less would serve than a broadly conceived plan and systematic agitation among the Jews. The deed resembles the actions perpetrated by the Russian terrorists of the 1870s who killed Aleksander II in that it achieved nothing. The consequences of Moses's deed, too, were similar: he, like most revolutionists in that situation, had to flee the country. Most revolutionists learn, by such experience, that isolated acts of aggression will not shake a firmly established system. Lenin fled to Switzerland. Mao Tse-tung eluded Chiang Kai-shek's blows against the Chinese Communist Party only because China was so vast and in such turmoil at the time. Moses fled to the land of Midian.

2. *Exile and God's Call*

Moses, first of the world's great revolutionists, was also the first great political exile. An outlaw now, he had no means of support. His attempt to help his people had ended in failure. For the moment, he was politically put out of action.

We must try to put ourselves in Moses's place: What was his mistake? How could he have succeeded? Was he to hate every Egyptian, and love every Jew? To the Jews he was bound by the ties of blood, and by his sympathy with the underdog; to the Egyptians, through his foster mother and his upbringing.

When he entered Midian, Moses came to a well. He saw young girls there, drawing water and pouring it into troughs for their animals to drink. A band of shepherds came up and tried to drive the women off, but Moses defended the women. Let us note that he was siding here with women who were total strangers to him, that he did so for no other reason than that they were too weak to defend themselves. Once again we see him casting his lot with the downtrodden, taking the side of the lowly. Thus Moses found a wife—one of the women he defended against the shepherds. His father-in-law was the priest of Midian. Moses would tend his sheep.

Life in exile was now bound to turn Moses's thoughts back to the country of his birth. In Midian, he was a foreigner. (The Mosaic law later would give extensive protection to guests.) His life as a shepherd left him ample time to think and ponder.

And then there came the moment that was a turning point in the world's history. On Mount Sinai Moses beheld a burning thornbush. He received his call at the very spot at which he was later to receive the decalogue. This was the burning thornbush that never turned to ashes. And out of the middle of the thornbush God called to Moses.

His numinous experience is probably to be interpreted as a dialogue between himself and the God of his conscience. His whole life, everything he had thought and done, reached its culmination in the fateful command that came to him on Mount Sinai. If we regard Moses's experience as a vision springing from his subconscious mind— which does not mean that we cannot also regard it as divinely ordained—we must ask ourselves why it was a burning thornbush that he saw. What does this burning thornbush symbolize? And what does the everlasting flame mean?

We find a most revealing clue in a source that deserves particular attention, precisely because it is so remote from Jewish history. Lenin, in the article "Where Do We Begin?," published in May 1901 in the fourth issue of *Iskra*, called for the "creation of an all-Russian newspaper" as the first practical step toward a nationwide revolutionary organization. Lenin's view was vigorously opposed by L. Nadeshdin in a pamphlet "On the Eve of the Revolution," which Lenin described as "the one and only attempt known to us that analyzes the question objectively." Lenin quoted Nadeshdin's arguments in their entirety in his famous book *What To Do?*. The pertinent passages quoted in Lenin's work include these sentences:

> "If we do not build up strong political organizations locally, what will be the use of even an excellently organized all-Russian newspaper? It will be a *burning bush, burning without being consumed*, and inflaming nobody."

Nadeshdin chose Moses's burning thornbush as a metaphor for the revolutionary impulse. In the framework of depth psychology, it is a valid interpretation. Flames are the symbol of the hot passion of love. Thorns symbolize resistance. Flaming resistance—this is the symbolic shape in which God appears to Moses.

We ought to avoid here the misapprehension that Nadeshdin's concluding phrase, "and inflaming nobody," invalidates the interpretation of the burning thornbush as a symbol of revolution. Not so. The phrase merely rejects the proposed newspaper (without a previously built up strong political organization, that is).

First, God proclaimed himself as the God of Abraham, Isaac, and Jacob, that is, the God of the Jews, who is wholly beyond any Egyptian hierarchy of gods. Next, he announced his divine purpose. He has

> come down to deliver them [the Israelites] out of the hand of the Egyptians, and to bring them up out of that land unto a good land and a large, unto a land flowing with milk and honey; unto the place of the Cannaanites. . . .
> Come now therefore, and I will send thee unto Pharaoh, that thou mayest bring forth my people the children of Israel out of Egypt.
> (Exodus 3:8, 10)

This command springing within Moses is like a thunderbolt leaping from those dark clouds that must have been gathering in his soul through all his years of exile. Let us posit here the questions that may have been crowding each other in his mind as he fled from Egypt, the dialogue that may have been obsessing him through his years of exile. And there was no precedent, no model to guide him.

Should he try to incite a general revolution in Egypt? He was as radically opposed to Egypt's iniquitous hierarchical system of pharaonism, especially its upper levels, as he was to Egypt's religion, which was little more than a justification of that system—the opium of the people. The worship of the God of Abraham was different. Had he not rejected human law when he demanded the sacrifice of Isaac? Had not Abraham surrendered the right of paternal dominance when he obeyed the Lord's command?

A violent overthrow of Egypt's government would have required the overthrow of the entire hierarchy of Egyptian gods—a practically hopeless undertaking. But Abraham's God, the one God, was he not above all hierarchies? Even to attempt such a revolution would have been irresponsible. The goals of such a revolution could be achieved only by a very long detour.

Should he try to liberate the Jews by taking them out of Egypt? Should he lead this people that had known slavery toward the establishment of a new society—a society that would be the seedbed of general revolution throughout the world? Their monotheism had already made them inimical to secular authority, as my interpretation of the sacrifice of Isaac may have shown. Could this ideology be developed into a system capable of successfully opposing the Egyptian religion, a religion that must surely have left its mark upon the Jews?

Could he guide the Jews to form a novel society distinguished by its truly humane organization? Were the Jews to commit themselves to a "subversive" principle of freedom in the midst of a society of slaves and slaveholders?

Did Moses indeed aim at such a universal revolution? Orthodox Jewish thought may not agree with us on the matter. But the definition of the Jewish nation as the "chosen people" could derive only from their peculiar fate in Egypt. Having experienced slavery and liberation, the Jews would be specially qualified and motivated to bring liberty to other nations.

Once Moses started seriously to think in terms of a Jewish exodus, he had to give thought to how the basic needs of such a society were to be satisfied. That nation could not hope to be welcomed anywhere with open arms. If the Jews were to organize themselves as a nomadic society they would have to fight unceasingly for the use of the rich pastures. Otherwise they would have to be content with lands that no one else wanted. In fact, they would be driven into the desert. But such a destination would be wholly incompatible with any attempt to establish a new society, one that, ultimately, would have to have a higher living standard than that of the old.

It was, then, only natural that Moses's mind turned to the possibility of conquering a fertile region. But it would have to be a region with a comparatively small population, because conquering a large country would have overtaxed by far the strength of the Jews.

We must, of course, raise this question: Did the Jews have the right to invade an alien country in which to set up their new society? Such an invasion would cost many lives. It is relatively simple for a group to choose to sacrifice the lives of its members for an ideal. But when that group demands sacrifices from others as well, the matter becomes extremely problematical. Were the Canaanites to suffer because the Jews had become slaves in Egypt?

Still, to assure the victory of the Mosaic revolution, the means for survival had to be found. The ideological message of that revolution was of such overriding significance for all mankind that Moses felt justified in demanding that not only the lives of Jews but also those of men of other nations be sacrificed for this idea.

We are faced here with one of the most difficult problems of the Mosaic revolution. Can we demand that human lives be sacrificed for spiritual values or for the advancement of mankind? For Moses, like for every revolutionist after him, the answer was yes. We cannot doubt that ultimately he hoped the commandment "Thou shalt not kill!" would prevail. But to achieve his goals he commanded "Thou shalt kill!" again and again. He regarded his first revolutionary act, the killing of the Egyptian who was beating a Jew, as an act of justice.

Moses was far too much of a realist not to be entirely aware, from the start, of the implications of his decision. For by now, he was no longer a hotheaded young terrorist.

Was there in fact a reasonable hope that the Jews could establish a home base from which a universal, egalitarian revolution might some day be launched?

And why was Moses destined to lead this revolution? Because his fate had placed him between two classes. He was a slave child raised to manhood close to the very peak of the Egyptian pyramid of power. A tremendous task thus fell upon his shoulders. The magnitude of what lay before him must have aroused in Moses inner resistance of like strength. Was he not bound to fight against it with every fiber of his being? To hesitate, draw back, and ask, Why must I be the one? Why can I not be left to tend my flocks in peace?

The final and compelling word from out of the burning thornbush, however, is said by the God of Moses's conscience, the holy spirit in history here speaking in God's name. (The concept that history is teleological, that a "world spirit," or, expressed theologically, the holy spirit, or God's will, moves toward its predestined goal, is no novel concept. The God in Exodus who refuses to define himself has been interpreted by a number of modern thinkers as a will that expresses itself through the workings of history. Among those who have developed historical theories accordingly are thinkers so diverse as Herder, Hegel, and Ranke, and the many others influenced by them. Also, Marxist socialism,

although embracing atheism, is rooted in messianic escha-
tology.) Moses was left with no choice. The imperative of
his conscience compelled him to accept the historic necessity. The Bible gives us a dramatic description of Moses's
inner struggle against that duty as well as prophesying his
future difficulties.

Moses revealed by his very first words that he was ready,
in body and soul, to meet the demand of history. One is
reminded of Abraham's reply when he was ordered to
sacrifice Isaac by Moses's response to God's call from out
of the burning bush: "Here am I" (Exodus 3:4).

His answer "Here am I" makes plain that he was ready,
that he was willing to disobey every human tradition and
give his sole obedience to God's call.

After commanding Moses to remove his shoes, for he was
standing on holy ground, the voice speaking to Moses iden-
tifies itself as "the God of thy father, the God of Abraham,
the God of Isaac, and the God of Jacob" (Exodus 3:6).
The voice informs Moses that the sorrows of his people are
known, that their cries from out of their oppression have
been heard. The time was now ripe for their deliverance
from Egypt and for their setting forth to "a good land and
a large, unto a land flowing with milk and honey. . ."
(Exodus 3:8).

God called Moses himself to be the one who would go
to Pharaoh and persuade him to release his entire population of Jewish slaves.

Everything that had gone through Moses's mind during
his exile now welled up once more in a mighty rush. His
doubts rushed up: "Who *am* I, that I should . . . bring forth
the children of Israel out of Egypt?" (Exodus 3:11).

God's response to these doubts is his promise, "Certainly
I will be with thee," and his command, "When thou hast
brought forth the people out of Egypt, ye shall serve God
upon this mountain" (Exodus 3:12).

This mountain of the burning thornbush is the mountain of the tablets of the law, the first law of the revolution. Here the first command was given; here the new law was later to be proclaimed. Eventual success was to give Moses the sense of having acted rightly.

Much later another revolutionary, one who seems unlikely to perform such an action, also climbed a holy mountain. Mao Tse-tung climbed Tai Shan, China's holiest mountain, after he had visited Confucius's grave. Mao was steeped in China's history. He doubtlessly knew that Liu Pang, the first emperor of the Han dynasty, had offered up a famous sacrifice at the grave of Confucius. Liu Pang, a revolutionist in the days when he was still tending the flocks, went on to conquer an empire. When Mao climbed Tai Shan, he was certainly aware that this was the place where the Han emperors had offered their sacrifices, and that they received their secret commands from the heavens on the highest peak of this mountain.

Mountaintops are frequently the places of revelation by virtue of their closeness to the sky and the vast view of the horizon they command.

The psychological problems that arise in every revolution do not stem solely from the psychic structure and thinking habits of the *ancien régime*'s ruling class. On the contrary: the very classes that are the bearers of the revolution are often far from being ripe for revolution. We know of Marx's lament that the proletariat found it so difficult to understand its own crucial importance for the society of the future.

Lenin, too, leaves no doubt that he expected the true revolutionary impetus to come from the ranks of the bourgeois intelligentsia, and that it was this sector of the bourgeoisie that must first awaken the proletariat to its historic mission. Only after the intelligentsia had succeeded in stirring up the masses, that social class which will carry the future, can the masses be moved to revolutionary action.

The slave mentality, however, is not easy to eradicate. It is perhaps most insidious among the kapos. When dealing with the Jewish kapos of Egypt, I realized the truth of a remark by Milovan Djilas in *The New Class*: "It has ever been the destiny of the slaves to provide their masters with the most intelligent and competent instruments of their masters' schemes."

One of Moses's greatest problems, perhaps *the* greatest, was that of bringing to the Jews the sense of their historic mission. He had to ask himself: Was he really the most suitable evangelist to persuade the Jews of this? For the Jews were sure to realize that, once they rebelled against the pharaonic hierarchy, their present state, secure though miserable, would come to an end, and from that moment forward they would be subjected to danger and sacrifice. The strongest resistance would surely come from among those who were profiting from the circumstances of their people: the kapos. They would point out the perils of the undertaking, and counsel "reason." They would urge that it was wiser to hold on to what they had rather than to lose everything, and that perhaps it would be more prudent to try to wrest a few concessions from the Egyptians than to make an all-out bid for freedom.

Moses, therefore, had to be prepared to wage battle on two fronts: the pharaonic system, and the resistance among the Jews themselves. Exodus 3:14–15 contains very specific instructions on what Moses was to tell the Jews. He was to invoke God's command. Moses himself was utterly convinced that he was in an absolute relation to the absolute, and that he must do what he will do because it is his duty toward God. In just that way, he must convince the Jews that their action is divinely willed, that they have a duty to perform and must take risks at God's command. In order to persuade them that the revolution is divinely ordained, God's absolute being is presented here in a passage as magnificent as any in the Bible:

> And Moses said unto God, Behold, *when* I come unto the children of Israel, and shall say unto them, The God of your fathers hath sent me unto you; and they shall say to me, What *is* his name? what shall I say unto them?
> And God said unto Moses, I AM THAT I AM.
>
> (Exodus 3:13–14)

Much has been written about this tautology, and about the fact that God, who has his being above and independent of all beings, refuses to define himself and instead appeals to the innermost core of every man, in a way that allows no doubt. He demands that man's faith rise to that absolute conviction that transcends human understanding and causes the believer to see himself as an executor of God's will.

This is the singularity of the Mosaic revolution: God's will. The Jews must carry it out, willing to make the highest sacrifices as Abraham was willing to sacrifice Isaac, as Moses himself is willing to undertake God's work.

> And God said moreover unto Moses, Thus shalt thou say unto the children of Israel, The Lord God of your fathers, the God of Abraham, the God of Isaac, and the God of Jacob, hath sent me unto you: this is my name for ever, and this *is* my memorial unto all generations.
>
> (Exodus 3:15)

This passage expresses Moses's basic ideology. The one God stands against the Egyptian hierarchy of deities, Moses against the pharaoh, the Jewish nation against Egypt, a new world rising up against the old.

Once we understand the supreme decision in Moses's conscience as a decision to obey God's command, we see also that his fight for the rights of man is the fight to carry out God's command.

The Bible passage just cited instructs Moses what to tell the Jews, and states what was to be the essence of Moses's motivation: The God of history commands!

The American revolution drew its strength from the same source: God has created all men *equal*. The French, the Russian, and the Chinese revolutions direct their appeal to purely human reason. But their fundamental principles are easily traced back to those of Moses. Concepts such as "universal reason" or "historical necessity" are hardly more than substitutes for the holy spirit.

The following Bible passages give a clear description of the tactics of the Mosaic revolution. The Jewish exodus begins with something like a strike for religious objectives:

> and thou shalt come, thou and the elders of Israel,
> unto the king of Egypt, and ye shall say unto him,
> The Lord God of the Hebrews hath met with
> us: and now let us go, we beseech thee, three days'
> journey into the wilderness, that we may sacrifice to
> the Lord our God.
>
> (Exodus 3:18)

The Bible immediately adds that the pharaoh will not be willing to let the Jews go "unless compelled by a mighty hand." (Exodus 3:19). His response was predictable. And the pharaoh is later reported as saying:

> Who *is* the Lord, that I should obey his voice
> to let Israel go? I know not the Lord, neither will
> I let Israel go.
>
> (Exodus 5:2)

It is only natural that the pharaoh should have reacted in that way. He could not be expected to submit to an authority other than that from which his own authority was derived, the hierarchy of the Egyptian gods. Where would bowing suddenly to another God lead him?

The pharaoh, however, immediately suspected an ulterior motive behind Moses's religious arguments: the Jews wanted to get out of working. He accused Moses and Aaron of inciting the Jews to strike:

> Wherefore do ye, Moses and Aaron, let the people
> from their works? get you unto your burdens . . .
> the people of the land now *are* many, and ye make
> them rest from their burdens.
> (Exodus 5:4–5)

It is true that Moses did consider slave labor an injustice. The God of the burning thornbush, the God of freedom, does not condone slave labor. Following his tenets means rejecting slavery. Accordingly, the Jews were not only to refuse to work as slaves in the future but were also to demand wages for their work done so far.

This position raises another moral problem that is crucial in all revolutions. Every revolution is "illegal" in the eyes of the established order. On hearing reports of revolution in Vienna an Austrian emperor is supposed to have exclaimed: "What! Do they have a permit for it?"

But matters are not so simple as the conservative minds of every age imagine. All conservatives are not bone-decent, staunch, reliable citizens; all revolutionists are not wicked, shiftless, evil criminals. In the duel between the pharaoh and Moses, or between Egypt and Israel, the pharaoh was indeed the respectable party upholding law and order, while Moses was the evildoer, the subversive character who "kept the people from their work," and who "upset everything," who "undermined" the Egyptian state, and "incited riot."

Actually, Moses did not want "lawlessness" any more

than did the pharaoh. He, too, based his case on "natural law"—but an entirely different one. He was acting out of a different frame of reference, a different basis in law. His God was a different God, and in that God's name he refused to accept Egyptian legality. Moses, too, wanted work for his people, but did not want them to do forced work. He was convinced that the prevailing system had upset all true relations between people and that it must now be reformed. He considered the Egyptian forced labor exploitation. His aim was not that of taking their right to economic gains away from the Egyptians. What he was trying to get were the wages they withheld unjustly from the Jews.

Concerning strikes for religious reasons, a veteran member of the Austrian Socialist Party once told me the following story. In the Austrian Empire before World War I, craftsmen's apprentices worked excessively long hours. Even on Sundays they had either to work or to attend their trade schools. Three and one half thousand years had gone by since Moses had come down from the mountain with the commandment, "Six days you shall work, but on the seventh day you shall rest." Yet the Austrian master craftsmen, most of them so-called Christians, refused to give their apprentices free Sundays. The socialists, at that time still illegal or semilegal, demanded, as a first step, that the apprentice be given a few hours' time on Sunday mornings, to "do his Sunday duty." A number of the masters looked upon this demand just as the pharaoh did: it was hypocritical, a sham-religious pretext for shirking work.

Those masters, however, were in a much weaker position than the pharaoh. They were being confronted by the socialists with genuine Christian principles that they supposedly had accepted, whereas the pharaoh laid claim to no principle of humanitarianism. Perhaps many of the

Austrian masters welcomed the passing of the law that compelled them to give free Sundays to their apprentices. We should keep in mind the fact that any enterprise is limited in its ability to make improvements by its need to remain competitive with other enterprises.

We now come to the most difficult part in the account of the Mosaic revolution, which is that of the problematic miracles by which Moses proved he was sent as an authentic messenger of God.

This much is certain: most modern men, Christians included, are very ill at ease with biblical reports of miracles. Rudolf Bultmann's effort to "demythologize" the Bible may be understood as an expression of this widespread tendency. Catholic exegesis is also frequently in line with this modern tendency by its willingness to define only some of these miracles as *contra naturam*. No objections were raised by the church to the attempt of the theologians to assign natural causes to an always growing number of accounts formerly considered miraculous.

A number of Moses's miracles can be explained in natural terms. Others might be explained, at best, only as magicians' tricks. This explanation gains in plausibility when we recall the biblical report that the Egyptian priests, too, performed similar deeds by their secret arts. (See Exodus 7:11.)

Let us remember that Moses was fully familiar with the pharaoh's thinking habits. The two men had probably been tutored together when they were children. And Moses himself had grown up in a world that believed in miracles. It would be natural to him to resort to magic as an expedient for weakening the pharaoh's defenses. Before examining those means, let us first take a look at the role of Aaron.

Moses does not consider himself sufficiently eloquent for the great task:

> And Moses said unto the Lord, O my Lord, I *am* not eloquent, neither heretofore, nor since thou has spoken unto thy servant: but I *am* slow of speech, and of a slow tongue.
>
> (Exodus 4:10)

The passage suggests a possible speech impediment, perhaps neurotic stuttering. Such a symptom might indicate sublimated aggression. Such an element in Moses's psychological make-up contains a clue to the symbolism of the burning thornbush. For a fleeting moment, Moses even makes an attempt to forget the entire mission:

> And he said, O my Lord, send, I pray thee, by the hand of *him whom* thou wilt send.
>
> And the anger of the Lord was kindled against Moses, and he said, *Is* not Aaron the Levite thy brother? I know that he can speak well. And also, behold, he cometh forth to meet thee; and when he seeth thee, he will be glad in his heart.
>
> (Exodus 4:13–14)

Moses needed a man who could act as agitator among the Israelites, and also as his negotiator with the pharaoh. His brother Aaron came to God's mind. The Levites, it seems, were to become the spokesmen of the Mosaic revolution and to develop a sense of solidarity based on their blood kinship with Moses. Aaron was to show himself a brilliant propagandist. But the real revolutionary initiative would still come from Moses.

After this dialogue with God, Moses left the land of Midian for Egypt, taking his wife and children with him. There is no indication, by the way, that Moses had a second wife. Despite his later acceptance of polygamy and divorce under the Mosaic law, Moses himself practiced monogamy.

There follows an exceedingly obscure passage in the biblical text:

> And it came to pass by the way in the inn, that the Lord met him, and sought to kill him.
>
> (Exodus 4:24)

It could mean a vision or a dream in which Moses was threatened by a superior, dangerous power, something like the final surfacing of his inner conflict before he faced his tremendous task.

Moses won Aaron over to his plan. Their first attempts to stir up the Jews were as successful as could be expected. It is easy to arouse men to revolutionary fervor. But when men encounter the first serious resistance, when the risks involved begin to impinge on the person, that fervor tends to cool.

So, also, with the Jews. When Moses and Aaron met with the pharaoh for the first time to begin the great struggle, the pharaoh, predictably, refused to concede to their demands. He, the supreme ruler, thought it an effrontery that he should be asked to allow a band of slaves to abandon their work in order to offer sacrifices to their own God. They simply did not want to work, they were lazy. Accordingly, he imposed harder working conditions: lazy people must be forced to work, coercion being the cure for laziness. If the slaves are kept busy enough, they will not listen to the seductive talk of rabble-rousers.

> Let there more work be laid upon the men, that they may labour therein; and let them not regard vain words.
>
> (Exodus 5:9)

We all know people who believe that Satan finds mischief for idle hands. Obediently, the Egyptian overseers increased the Jews' work quota. But the Jewish kapos were unable to browbeat the men into meeting the new quota. They went to the pharaoh to complain, but he did not relent.

After their return from the audience with the pharaoh, the kapos met Moses and Aaron. Their resentment, quite understandably, now turned against these two—the trouble-makers. They accused Moses and Aaron of being responsible for the people's plight; and in terms of the prevailing system, they were right.

Moses and Aaron responded by stepping up their agitation. They promised that God will establish a covenant with the Jewish people, that he will give them the land of Canaan, and that they will be free.

Then the counteragitation of the Jewish kapos, together with the measures taken by the pharaoh, began to take effect. Moses ran into serious difficulties. The slaves wished to enjoy the sweet fruits of freedom, to be sure; but they did not want to fight for freedom. Moses realized he was failing:

> And Moses spake before the Lord, saying, Behold, the children of Israel have not hearkened unto me; how then shall Pharaoh hear me, who *am* of uncircumsized lips?
> And the Lord said unto Moses, See, I have made thee a god to Pharaoh: and Aaron thy brother shall be thy prophet.
>
> (Exodus 6:12; 7:1)

To be effective then, Moses must be endowed with godlike authority. The pharaoh must be brought to regard him as a god, and Aaron as the god's instrument. All potentates like the pharaoh are basically insecure because they sense how questionable their right to power is. Thus they are unusually subject to the fear of others having a divine mandate. Herod did not dare kill John the Baptist, probably because he was impressed by the conviction ringing in John the Baptist's words, until Salome overcame his hesitation. And when Herod was told that Jesus spoke "as one with authority" he felt apprehensive about him.

Moses, then, to carry conviction, had to appear before the pharaoh clothed in godlike authority. It was the miracles that endowed Moses with the authority he needed. After a series of plagues, the pharaoh was ready to negotiate. He offered to let the Jewish men go, but stipulated that the women and children must stay behind. When Moses rejected this condition, the pharaoh accused him of "some evil purpose." He suspected, rightly, that the Jews had no intention of returning.

Another plague. The pharaoh was ready to make further concession. This time he demanded that only the cattle of the Jews be left behind. The cattle, however, represented the economic basis for the exodus. Again Moses refused, offering religious arguments. And then for the first time the pharaoh threatened Moses's life:

> And Pharaoh said unto him, Get thee from me, take heed to thyself, see my face no more; for in *that* day thou seest my face thou shalt die.
>
> (Exodus 10:28)

The fact that the pharaoh was willing to tolerate Moses's conduct up to this point must be ascribed to Moses's powerful personality. Besides, the two may have been friends as children. Matters had to reach an extreme point before the pharaoh was willing to overcome his reluctance to use force against Moses.

3. The Killing of the First-born and the Passover Lamb

Abraham's sacrifice of Isaac, a sacrifice fully consummated only in Abraham's mind, was followed by the actual slaying of the ram. The death of the first-born among the Egyptians was mirrored by the killing of the lambs among the Jews. Jesus died in man's stead. Thus unfolded within the framework of Judaism the mighty drama of human liberation.

But let us return once more to the pharaoh and Moses.

A terrible event was then announced by Moses, the last, conclusive scourge that was to force the pharaoh to allow the Jews to leave Egypt. All pretense that they would leave only temporarily, to offer sacrifices, was by then abandoned. If that event did take place with all the severity reported in the Bible, its effect must have been horrifying. Moses announced God's decision:

> And Moses said, Thus saith the Lord, About midnight will I go out into the midst of Egypt:
> And all the firstborn in the land of Egypt shall die, from the firstborn of Pharaoh that sitteth upon his throne, even unto the firstborn of the maidservant that *is* behind the mill; and all the firstborn of beasts. . . .
> But against any of the children of Israel shall not a dog move his tongue, against man or beast: that ye may know how that the Lord doth put a difference between the Egyptians and Israel.
> (Exodus 11:4–5, 7)

Things that happen for the first time assume a special significance. A woman's first birth is the hardest; her first-born child, borne in the greatest pain, is loved with a special love. And his death would bring unequaled pain.

God, the supreme Father, had commanded, but the pharaoh refused to obey him. The pharaoh was not willing to give his subjects freedom. In consequence, his first-born and the first-born of every Egyptian lost their lives. The first-born of the Jews were not slain, however, because the Jews obeyed the command of God, the command of history, which the conservative Egyptians did not.

Every revolution is a conflict between father and son. The pharaoh, too, is a secondary father figure and paternal authority.

The Jews, as evidence of their willingness to offer sacrifice, were ordered to offer up a lamb, as Abraham was ordered to offer up Isaac. It is of great significance that they symbolically demonstrated their willingness to sacrifice their first-born to God, to place them under God's immediate jurisdiction, so that they had to buy their lives with the offering of a lamb or, if they were very poor, of a pigeon. All first-born had to be set free by sacrifice. All fathers and mothers had to offer up their Isaacs to God in the same way; they had to be willing to set aside their own desires.

Thus the paschal lamb has become the perennial symbol of freedom. It is a constant reminder that we must obey God's will—and, therefore, must disobey the will of man when necessary. It is a reminder that the first-born of the Egyptians were slain so that the freedom of the enslaved Jews might be procured. It is a symbol of man's willingness to make revolution, and to accept the consequences of his resistance to human authority.

Unleavened and unsalted bread also became part of Jewish ritual at that time. It was the bread of the Egyptian slaves, it is a reminder of their bondage. It is a symbol of bondage just as the sacrifice of the lamb, substitute for the first-born, is a symbol of freedom. The lamb's blood on the doorpost was the sign for the destroyer angel to pass by.

> And Pharaoh rose up in the night, he, and all his servants, and all the Egyptians; and there was a great cry in Egypt; for *there was* not a house where *there was* not one dead.
>
> (Exodus 12:30)

It cannot surprise us that the Pharaoh was so deeply shaken by the event that he gave in and allowed the Jews to leave Egypt. But we must also understand that he inevitably conceived a tremendous hatred of the Jews. That this "filth of a people" had broken his will was an unheard-of humiliation for him. It shook the very foundations of his world, the absolute authority of the Egyptian hierarchy of gods. Indeed, his own unyielding attitude up to this point is understandable only in terms of his position within that hierarchy.

His final request shows how deeply he was affected:

> and be gone; and bless me also.
>
> (Exodus 12:32)

Thus the exodus began, and at its very start, Moses revealed its egalitarian principle:

> One law shall be to him that is homeborn, and unto the stranger that sojourneth among you.
>
> (Exodus 12:49)

4. The Exodus and the Law of Revolution

In keeping with the inner logic of symbols, the Jews, after the exodus, held all first-born in special veneration, because the death of the Egyptian first-born had thrown open to them the gates of freedom. The day they escaped from their slavery was to be kept in memory forever and was established as one of their holiest days. It lives on in the Easter feast of the Christian calendar. It was at the Passover supper, which was to become known in Christianity as the last supper, that Jesus, shortly before his death on the cross, gave his apostles the eucharist. And he elected to die on the first day of Passover.

Henceforth all first-born male children had, so to speak, to be ransomed from God:

> And it shall be when thy son asketh thee in time to come, saying, What *is* this? that thou shalt say unto him, By strength of hand the Lord brought us out from Egypt, from the house of bondage:
> And it came to pass, when Pharaoh would hardly let us go, that the Lord slew all the firstborn in the land of Egypt, both the firstborn of man, and the

> firstborn of beast: therefore I sacrifice to the Lord
> all that openeth the matrix, being males; but all the
> firstborn of my children I redeem.
> And it shall be for a token upon thine hand, and
> for frontlets between thine eyes; for by strength of
> hand the Lord brought us forth out of Egypt.
> (Exodus 13:14–16)

Another item of fundamental psychological significance
should be noted. The eruption of the Jewish nation out of
Egypt is analogous to childbirth. Lenin, too, compared a
revolution to a birth. The Jewish nation, like a first-born
who "opens the womb," burst forth from the vast womb
of Egyptian society, and Egyptian blood flowed in the
process.

We shall see how immature this nation of slaves was at
that time. Moses knew it well; he had experienced their
vacillations. He therefore did not lead them out of Egypt
by the shortest route,

> Lest peradventure the people repent when they see
> war, and they return to Egypt.
> (Exodus 13:17)

Thus did Moses acknowledge the Jews' fear of the
hardships that accompany independence and responsibility. Then he met more resistance. The pharaoh became
enraged after the Jews had departed, and tried to bring
them back. Moses in turn had to listen once more to his
people's accusations:

> Is not this the word that we did tell thee in Egypt,
> saying, Let us alone, that we may serve the Egyp-
> tians? For it had been better for us to serve the
> Egyptians, than that we should die in the wilderness.
> (Exodus 14:12)

The winds prevailing in the northern reaches of the Red
Sea often cause the waters to recede. Apparently this
phenomenon occurred also at the time of the exodus, a
circumstance that favored the migration of the Jews. When

the water receded, the Jews set out on their journey. They passed through the sea of reeds and reached the far shore. When the pharaoh's troops were coming in pursuit, the waters returned.

Their dramatic escape through the Red Sea cut the Jews off, and set them free to face a new life of independence. But their new life, without protection and exposed to every danger, was uncertain and perilous. Disgruntled by the privations of desert life, they turned against Moses and Aaron. Their former life in Egypt—they were enslaved, yes, but they were free from responsibilities—appeared to them now in a new light:

> Would to God we had died by the hand of the Lord in the land of Egypt, when we sat by the flesh pots, *and* when we did eat bread to the full, for ye have brought us forth into this wilderness, to kill this whole assembly with hunger.
>
> (Exodus 16:3)

All peoples hurl such accusations at their revolutionary leaders as soon as their first revolutionary acts involve hardships. But neither the American nor the French nor the Russian revolutions could improve the situation of the people overnight. Far from it. A period of hardships when things are worse than they had been before inevitably follows upon the start of every revolution. During that period, the whole burden of responsibility weighs upon the revolutionary leaders. They are forced to go on waging war on two fronts: against the circumstances that surround them, and against their own people.

In a similar situation—when the American revolution was at a low—Tom Paine wrote:

> These are the times that try men's souls. The summer soldier and the sunshine patriot will, in this crisis, shrink from the service of their country; but

he that stands it now, deserves the love and thanks of man and woman. Tyranny, like hell, is not easily conquered; yet we have this consolation with us, that the harder the conflict, the more glorious the triumph. What we obtain too cheap, we esteem too lightly: it is dearness only that gives every thing its value. Heaven knows how to put a proper price upon its goods; and it would be strange indeed if so celestial an article as freedom should not be highly rated. . . .

Let it be told to the future world, that in the depth of winter, when nothing but hope and virtue could survive, that the city and the country, alarmed at one common danger, came forth to meet and to repulse it. It matters not where you live, or what rank of life you hold, the evil or the blessing will reach you all. The far and the near, the home counties and the back, the rich and the poor, will suffer or rejoice alike. The heart that feels not now is dead; the blood of his children will curse his cowardice, who shrinks back at a time when a little might have saved the whole, and made *them* happy. I love the man that can smile in trouble, that can gather strength from distress, and grow brave by reflection. 'Tis the business of little minds to shrink; but he whose heart is firm, and whose conscience approves his conduct, will pursue his principles unto death. My own line of reasoning is to myself as straight and clear as a ray of light . . . I thank God, that I fear not. I see no real cause for fear. I know the situation well, and can see the way out of it. By perserverance and fortitude we have the prospect of a glorious issue; by cowardice and submission, the sad choice of a variety of evils—a ravaged country— a depopulated city—habitations without safety, and slavery without hope—our homes turned into barracks and bawdy houses for Hessians, and a future race to provide for, whose fathers we shall doubt of. Look on this picture and weep over it! and if there yet remains one thoughtless wretch who believes it not, let him suffer it unlamented.

These words could have been spoken by Moses to the Jewish people. Similar passages can readily be found in the writings of Lenin and other leaders of revolution; the initial, seemingly easy victories are always followed by times to try men's souls. The trials of the Jews began immediately after their departure from Egypt.

In the desert the Jews sustained themselves by the manna brought by the night wind. During his exile in the land of Midian, Moses had learned how to survive in the desert.

The day was not long in coming when the Jews had to fight. Their incursion into alien countries was beginning. An army had to be formed, a commander appointed. Moses found a capable military leader in Joshua. Himself a civilian, Joshua selected men untried in battle but filled with courage, and with them he defeated the Amalekites.

This event, too, is typical of revolutions. The armies of the revolution do win out over the battle-tested troops of the *ancien régime*. Commanders arise—writers like Trotsky, or poets like Mao Tse-tung—who prove themselves superior to the professionals, in Russia to the White Russian generals, in China to career officers such as Chiang Kai-shek, who had himself been trained by German generals (among them General von Seeckt). True, the American revolutionary army had a well-trained leader in George Washington, but the troops were largely inexperienced men. The ultimate superiority of revolutionary armies rests on their absolute moral commitment to their cause. Besides, their leaders, unhampered in mind by the traditions of military academies, are infinitely more flexible than the generals and their forces who resist revolution. It is a matter of profound regret that the Bible tells us nothing about Joshua's initial strategy and tactics.

Moses then organized the Jews into groups to lighten his own burden. He also began to promulgate his first laws.

But the decisive legislation, by which the life of the new society was henceforth to be guided, did not begin until the Jews had reached Mount Sinai, the mountain on which Moses had received the call to revolution. Here the Jews are assigned their special role:

> Then ye shall be a peculiar treasure unto me above all people: for all the earth *is* mine:
> And ye shall be unto me a kingdom of priests, and an holy nation.
>
> (Exodus 19:5–6)

The fundamental meaning of the election of the Jews as the chosen people rings in these words. This nation is to be an "elite" in the world.

During a thunderstorm Moses went up to Mount Sinai and there received the decalogue, which is surely the first revolutionary body of law in history. It is the moral constitution of a decent world. No other revolution has even remotely approached that achievement. It will be well to study this legislation more closely.

Its essence lies in the Lord's first commandment:

> I *am* the Lord thy God, which have brought thee out of the land of Egypt, out of the house of bondage.
>
> (Exodus 20:2)

In this self-proclamation, God, the God of the burning thornbush and of the thunderstorm over Mount Sinai, revealed himself as the God of freedom, the God who loathes bondage. Here is the archetypal litany of the Jewish people. Out of these words has grown the twisted branches of antisemitism; they also are the source of the Jews' revolutionary drive, which is so troublesome to the fascist mind. A people in whose ears the words "the house of bondage" have been ringing for more than three thousand years—such a people must love freedom above anything else in the world. And in this fact lies the Jews' greatest contribution to human civilization, a contribution that is appreciated far too little.

Those who exalt the classical age of Greece and Rome above all other civilizations commit one mistake: they grossly underrate this contribution of the Jews to the progress of mankind.

In part, that underestimation stems from the focus on the spiritual that usually prevails in the study of Jewish history. We tend to act as though the history of the Jews were simply not a part of world history because it is the predecessor of the history of Christianity. A different view should now be taken, one in which we see every event in Jewish history as true history as well as action directed by God. Jesus was fully human; just so, the history of Christianity is also human history in the full sense.

The next sentence of the first commandment is at its core religious but is also fraught with social implications:

> Thou shalt have no other gods before me.
>
> (Exodus 20:3)

A God who stands in an immediate relation to every single human individual is an enormous force for equality, for egalitarianism. All antiegalitarian societies that adopt monotheism sense the profound contradiction lying at their very heart. All images or likenesses of God are outlawed in the commandments in order to counteract the possible resurgence of polytheism. God is a jealous God; he will not tolerate other gods before him. His very name is holy.

And holy, too, is God's day, on which no work is to be done. Moses's third commandment is the first law in history to order man to have free time. Even the domestic animals are protected against exploitation. Let us note that this law did not place too heavy a burden on a society whose consumer needs were so modest. But whatever the need of modern society for high productivity, the fight for the eight-hour day is as nothing compared with this first institution of one free day each week!

The free time legislated in the third commandment, incidentally, has to this day retained its function: it is a time to face God (or, in secular terms, to think about life's meaning), to concentrate on cultivating one's humanity, and to catch one's breath.

The force and power of this legislation is totally without parallel. Impressive as the Roman law is in many ways, it pales in comparison with the decalogue.

In justice, we must note that in his later laws Moses did not always adhere to egalitarian standards. In the Mosaic law, slaves are persons, to be sure, not objects as in Roman law. But Moses did not end slavery or give equal rights to women. He allowed divorce and polygamy. Nor were other peoples placed on the same footing with the Jews.

All this is true. These are facts. We may explain them by saying that Moses settled for doing as much as was possible. But when one calls to mind Moses's own greatness, and his God's claim to rule over all nations, one may perhaps surmise that there lay beyond these laws a plan of vastly greater scope, making it necessary to compromise for a time rather than seriously to endanger the new direction of man.

One proof of this is Jesus's comment on at least one Mosaic law that is imperfect. Jesus, who said of himself that he had come to fulfill the law, spoke of the problem of divorce as follows:

> Wherefore they are no more twain, but one flesh. What therefore God hath joined together, let not man put asunder.
> They say unto him, Why did Moses then com-

mand to give a writing of divorcement, and to put
her away?

He saith unto them, Moses because of the hard-
ness of your hearts suffered you to put away your
wives: but from the beginning it was not so.

And I say unto you. . . .

(Matthew 19:6–9)

What is noteworthy here is less the question of divorce
itself than the exegesis Jesus gave of Moses's intentions.
For he states unequivocally that Moses had the objective
of protecting women but that his law went only halfway,
because he had to compromise with the attitudes of his
day. Jesus, taking up where Moses left off, fulfills the
spirit, not just the letter, of the Mosaic law, and he is fully
conscious of continuing in the Mosaic tradition.

We may add further to our understanding of Moses by
comparing him with other revolutionists. The American
Declaration of Independence, for example, the basic document of the American revolution, proclaimed that "all
men are created equal." Yet slavery survived in the United
States for almost another century. Nevertheless, in the
long run the Declaration has exerted a decisive influence.
The northern abolitionists began to invoke it, then to demand it be enforced. The process of enforcing equality for
Negroes is still being carried on today. In 1855, Abraham
Lincoln, in a letter, wrote: "As a nation, we began by
declaring that '*all men are created equal.*' We now
practically read it 'all men are created equal, *except
negroes.*' "

Clearly, then, revolutionary principles need time to become transformed into reality, even after a powerful start.
The Declaration of Independence is not a hypocritical
document, although its principles have taken time, and are
still taking time, to become realities.

Even the Russian revolution shows this shift. When it
became clear to the Russian leaders that the world revolu-

tion could not be launched immediately after the success of the Soviet revolution, they proclaimed the establishment of "socialism in one country." Moses's restriction of his revolution to the Jews is analogous. But neither restriction was final.

5. The Counterrevolution and Its Liquidation

Moses's choice of young bulls as a sacrificial peace offering to the God of the Jews may be understood as a symbolic gesture. The bull was then regarded as a symbol of Egypt's religion. A sacrifice of bulls to the God of the Jews during the exodus is to be interpreted as severing ties with conservation. Those who lost faith in Moses and believed they would have to return to Egypt gathered around the former kapos because they believed they would again have power. The exodus had deprived the kapos of their privileged position in the Egyptian system, a fact that inevitably made them Moses's antagonists.

With Joshua, whom he had singled out to become his successor, Moses withdrew onto Mount Sinai and there remained for forty days and nights. It was to be expected that his absence would lend fresh impetus to the counterrevolutionary forces. When Moses was not present the revolution of the Jews was without its soul. Even his closest supporters lacked his charisma and skill as revolutionary evangelist. If the kapos were to make an attempt to seize power, the time for it to be made was obviously during Moses's absence.

The counterrevolutionary attempt also had a religious aspect. To exalt the bull, sacred symbol of the Egyptian religion, and give it divine status would be tantamount to a relapse into that religion.

We must, of course, keep in mind, that even if the

Egyptian bull had become the central symbol of a regres-
sive religion, and even if the former kapos had seized
power, the conditions of the Jews that prevailed in Egypt
could not have been restored. The political power would
have been in the hands of Jews who were, one might say,
imitators of the Egyptians, what we shall call secondary-
Egyptians. By this interpretation, the Jewish faction who
made the golden calf becomes essentially a fascist party.
Regression to the ideology of an earlier age and to the corresponding forms of political rule and power structure is
typical of fascism. The leaders of fascism, however, do not
usually stem from the former ruling class. They merely
imitate the former masters. National Socialism was a
secondary feudalism of the petite bourgeoisie with an ideological regression to Old Germanic mythology.

The leaders of the anti-Mosaic revolution, then, were
Jewish secondary-Egyptians who relapsed into Egyptian
notions of political rule and Egyptian religion. One could
make a case for them as reactionaries as analogous in many
ways to the Nazis.

Apparently they constituted a real danger. In any case,
Aaron's conduct toward them presents us with a number
of riddles. Aaron, we recall, took an active part himself in
the making of the golden calf. Moses, returning from the
mountain with the stone tablets of the new law, was out-
raged by the Jews' backsliding. He blamed Aaron, who put
up only a feeble defense. Moses then gathered his followers together:

> Who is on the Lord's side? let him come unto me.
> (Exodus 32:26)

The Levites gathered around and Moses gave them a
terrible command:

> Thus saith the Lord God of Israel, Put every man
> his sword by his side, and go in and out from gate to
> gate throughout the camp, and slay every man his

brother, and every man his companion, and every man his neighbour.

And the children of Levi did according to the word of Moses: and there fell of the people that day about three thousand men.

For Moses had said, Consecrate yourself to-day to the Lord, even every man upon his son, and upon his brother; that he may bestow upon you a blessing this day.

(Exodus 32:27–29)

This action definitively broke the back of the opposition. Moses and his Levite swords had crushed the counterrevolutionary cadre.

Much later, Jesus was to declare with equal inexorability:

Think not that I am come to send peace on earth: I come not to send peace, but a sword.

For I am come to set a man at variance against his father, and the daughter against her mother, and the daughter in law against her mother in law.

And a man's foes shall be they of his own household.

He that loveth father or mother more than me is not worthy of me: and he that loveth son or daughter more than me is not worthy of me.

And he that taketh not his cross, and followeth after me is not worthy of me.

He that findeth his life shall lose it: and he that loseth his life for my sake shall find it.

(Matthew 10:34–39)

The central idea of the Mosaic revolution is so supreme that it may call, if need be, for the sacrifice even of one's own closest kin. By slaying their own relatives, Moses held, the Levites had "ordained themselves for the service of the Lord." Jesus never disagreed with Moses on this point. On the contrary, he seems to have been just as radical himself. The destruction of three thousand lives at the very foot of the mountain on which God had appeared in the burning thornbush, an act of terrorism unleashed by Moses, did not prevent Jesus from appearing on Mount Tabor by the side of Elijah and Moses.

The essential point here is that the so-called natural ties —the bonds of kinship, nation, and the like—must give way before the claims of the community of spirit. This fact is slowly coming to be understood today. Caucasians feel much closer, after all, to a peace-loving black or Indian or Chinese than to any German, Austrian, or American fascist who is willing to kill a man because of his skin color. This community of the spirit, transcending all biological relations, is Mosaic—and it is also Christian.

Although the counterrevolution had been crushed, the Mosaic revolution had not yet attained even its short-range goals. Infinite labors lay ahead.

6. Israel's Long March and the Establishment of the New Order

Now that the new law had been made secure, Moses undertook his first tentative move against the land of Canaan. He sent out scouts to reconnoitre. They returned with the intelligence that the country was strongly defended; most of them did not give the Jews a chance to conquer it. And once again this nation of slaves began to whimper:

> And all the children of Israel murmured against Moses and against Aaron; and the whole congregation said unto them, Would God that we had died in the land of Egypt! or would God we had died in this wilderness!
> And wherefore hath the Lord brought us unto this land, to fall by the sword, that our wives and our children should be a prey? were it not better for us to return into Egypt?
> (Numbers 14:2-3)

But their military leader Joshua, the future conqueror of Canaan, and others with him, were ready to attack. They thus brought down upon themselves such enmity that they came near to being stoned to death by the people. Then the Lord told Moses and Aaron that the people were to be told the following words:

> Your carcases shall fall in this wilderness; and all that were numbered of you, according to your whole number, from twenty years old and upward, which have murmured against me.
> Doubtless ye shall not come into the land, concerning which I sware to make you dwell therein, . . .
> But your little ones, which ye said should be a prey, them will I bring in, and they shall know the land which ye have despised.
> But as for you, your carcases, they shall fall in this wilderness.
> And your children shall wander in the wilderness forty years, and bear your whoredoms, until your carcases be wasted in the wilderness.
> (Numbers 14:29-33)

Moses had decided to take a long road. A generation of men, all those whose minds had been molded by Egyptian servitude, were to die, or at least, their number was to be greatly reduced, so that they were no longer numerous enough to sway the community:

> I the Lord have said, I will surely do it unto all this evil congregation, that are gathered together against me: in this wilderness they shall be consumed, and there they shall die.
> (Numbers 14:35)

A new generation would grow up during these forty years. They would be men who had not known slavery and therefore could dream no tearful, sentimental fantasies of the good old days. They would decide what direction the new society was to take, and would be strong enough to set it up on firm foundations.

Moses's portentous decree is of extreme severity and of supreme realism. No other decision Moses made reveals as clearly and compellingly how earnest was his effort, how serious his purpose. To serve his revolutionary aims, he sacrificed two generations. Every revolution needs such a period of forty years to become fully established.

Reactionary voices never tire of telling us that this or that revolutionary aim is "utopian" and "against human nature" because "people are the way they are" and more of the same. Many Egyptians must have told Moses: "With such a people of slaves, do you propose to build a nation of free men, based on entirely different principles? These people need the strong hand of a master. Their slavish mentality is passed on from generation to generation in the same way as is the mentality of the masters. There are 'natural' masters, and there are 'natural' slaves."

And indeed, did not Moses's own experience with his people confirm these warnings? Did not his people show their slave mentalities? We must admit that those reactionary objections contain a kernel of truth. But they have only limited validity.

It is true that a slave does not become a free man simply by being set at liberty. Noble ideas are conceived more easily than they are transformed into reality. But it is simply not true that nothing can ever be changed.

This decision—to postpone the realization of his great longing for forty years filled with hardship—may well have been the most cruelly difficult decision Moses ever made, but he acted upon the kernel of truth that the reactionaries are always reciting. Forty years, he thought, was the time needed for the great process of reeducation. These forty years constituted actually the true saga of Jewish heroism. They are the years of the long march.

Men are made into slaves not by heredity but by the

habits bred into them in their childhood. Reeducation later on can do much to change those early implanted habits. It can be done if one goes about it in earnest, though it is neither so easy as many well-meaning socialist dreamers would have us believe nor as impossible as reactionaries warn.

This decision more than any other establishes Moses as one of history's greatest figures, one of the truest messengers of God's will on this earth. He did not chose the easy road—not for himself nor for his people. But he laid the firm foundation for all future revolutions.

Forty more years. Then the Jews would conquer Canaan. Then the Jews would be able to take a breath. The liberalization could begin.

Forty years. The extreme rigor of the reeducation of the Jews was bound to bring to the fore the kind of men who would insist on quick solutions, impatient men for whom the revolution was not moving fast enough. The rebellion of Korah and his company doubtless was such a left-wing deviationist movement.

Korah, a Levite, that is a member of the vanguard of the Mosaic revolution, rebelled against Moses. It is not hard to sympathize with the charges Korah made: he accused Moses of overreaching himself, of promoting a cult of personality, and thus violating the egalitarian thrust of the revolutionary goals:

> And they gathered themselves together against Moses and against Aaron, and said unto them, Ye take too much upon you, seeing all the congregation are holy, every one of them, and the Lord is among them: wherefore then lift ye up yourselves above the congregation of the Lord?
>
> (Number 16:3)

The accusation is specific and accurate. All of the Jews, the whole congregation, were chosen. But was not Moses in his position as their permanent leader not just another pharaoh? And was not Korah the true representative of the revolutionary idea? Thoughts such as these prompted Korah to refuse obedience to Moses in the name of the revolution.

What we observe here is not a counterrevolutionary deviation to the right, as with the faction who made the golden calf, but a deviation to the left. Korah and his men wanted to achieve the revolutionary goals at once; they refused to understand that there is need for a period of transition.

The biblical report also makes it clear that Korah's faction objected to the delay of the conquest of Canaan. They blamed Moses not only for his cult of personality, but also accused him of slackness:

> We will not come up: Is it a small thing that thou hast brought us up out of a land that floweth with milk and honey, to kill us in the wilderness, except thou make thyself altogether a prince over us?
> (Numbers 16:12–13)

To accuse Moses of having brought them out of the promised land was sheer demagoguery. What he had done was to refuse to lead them into that land at that time, which is hardly the same thing. In any event, they objected to Moses's position of eminence. They wanted to establish an egalitarian democracy at that very moment.

The analogies between Moses's position and that of the pharaoh, however, led them to overlook the fundamental differences between those two men. The pharaoh intended his rule and that of his heirs to be permanent, while Moses looked upon himself merely as a transitional leader. Moses thought it his function to render his position superfluous, but that could be achieved only by reeducating the Jews.

This short-sightedness of Korah's rebellion is typical of

left-wing deviationist sectarians and adventurers, as they are called in the communist vocabulary. Everything that is said by Mao Tse-tung in his essay "On Protracted War," all his arguments against deviation to the right or the left, can equally be applied to the deviationism in the Mosaic revolution. Mao speaks out against two mistaken views concerning the Sino-Japanese War. In his opinion (and events proved him right) the "theory of China's inevitable subjugation" was just as wrong as the "theory of China's quick victory."

Transposed into the context of the Mosaic revolution, the "theory of China's inevitable subjugation" corresponds to the wish of the Jews to return to Egypt and to bondage to the pharaoh. This is the right-wing "surrender mentality" of those Israelites who adopted the reactionary theory that Jews were natural slaves, forever incapable of victory.

Conversely, the "theory of quick victory" corresponds to the activism of Korah's faction. Canaan was held by a strong people. Reeducation of the Jews, and ample war preparations—both were essential. To attack Canaan without them would have been what Mao called "adventurism."

Besides, though Moses held firmly to the principle that all men are equal before the Lord, he felt he had to delay democratization, and keep the reins in his own hands, until such time as the Jewish nation's reeducation was realized. He had to remain as the central force for equilibrium and reason until the Jewish nation achieved its own inner balance.

In these considerations lie the explanation of Moses's drastic action against Korah's rebellion. He liquidated Korah and his men, just as he had liquidated the counterrevolution of the faction who made the golden calf. Again, the objectives of the Mosaic revolution were his justification. Left-wing deviationism is just as deadly a peril to revolutionary aims as right-wing deviationism.

The deviationists of the right cast doubt upon the revolutionary goals, while those of the left, by their extreme radicalism and constant pressure for the instant realization of their goals, threaten the progress of the revolution itself and cause it to fail.

In passing, I would like to point out, in view of the often mythological language of the biblical account, that those flames that destroyed Korah and his men may have been a symbol of that fury with which the Jewish nation swept two hundred and fifty men to their death.

I shall not comment on the several wars which the Mosaic revolution became involved in, or on the purification that the Jews underwent through these wars. After forty years, their reeducation was accomplished. A new generation had grown to manhood, one that saw the fleshpots of Egypt as only sentimental nostalgia of the old folks bemoaning the good old days. The countless sacrifices made for freedom's sake had forged a new nation, hardened and ready to assume responsibility for its own destiny. The work of Moses's life was accomplished.

The Jewish nation girded itself for the conquest of the land on which the new society could entrench itself firmly. And Moses, satisfied that the nation had in Joshua an able military leader, died. Moses was surely one of the greatest, most valiant, most daring men in history.

> And there arose not a prophet since in Israel like unto Moses, whom the Lord knew face to face,
> In all the signs and the wonders, which the Lord sent him to do in the land of Egypt to Pharaoh, and to all his servants, and to all his land,
> And in all that mighty hand, and in all the great terror which Moses shewed in the sight of all Israel.
> (Deuteronomy 34:10–12)

III.

═══════════════════════════════════════

THE STRUGGLE AGAINST SECONDARY
PHARAONISM: THE PROPHETS
AND KINGS OF ISRAEL

The Lord shall rule over you.
—Gideon, according to the Book of Judges (8:23)

THE HISTORY of the Jews after Moses has been reported
from two opposing points of view: that of the progressives,
who took their stand against the kings and held with the
old prophets, and that of the reactionaries, lackeys, and
sycophants of the kings.

The line of the prophetic tradition that leads from
Moses to Jesus is straight and unmistakable. From Moses
it led to Gideon and Samuel, to Elijah, and to John the
Baptist, whose head was severed by Herod's executioners.
And it continued on to Jesus, whose struggle against the
ecclesiastical establishment ended upon the cross.

This is the line that I shall trace in the present work,
because the prophets are the true, authentic contribution
of the Jews to the history of mankind.

In Chapter 5 of Deuteronomy, the narrative repeats
once more the decalogue that God spoke while "the mountain did burn with fire" (Deuteronomy 5:23). In Chapter 6, the account rises to still loftier heights. Here is pro-

claimed that one commandment—commandment, be it
noted, not prohibition—that Jesus called the greatest of
all:

> Hear, O Israel: The Lord our God is one Lord:
>   And thou shalt love the Lord thy God with all
> thine heart, and with all thy soul, and with all
> thy might.
>
> (Deuteronomy 6:4–5)

The decalogue is Moses's greatest and ultimate legacy.

> And these words, which I command thee this day,
> shall be in thine heart:
>   And thou shalt teach them diligently unto thy
> children, and shalt talk of them when thou sittest
> in thine house, and when thou walkest by the way,
> and when thou liest down, and when thou risest up.
>   And thou shalt bind them for a sign upon thine
> hand, and they shall be as frontlets between thine
> eyes.
>   And thou shalt write them upon the posts of thy
> house, and on thy gates.
>
> (Deuteronomy 6:6–9)

With this ideological bequest Moses has exercised profound influence upon all future history. His realization
that the love of God abiding in a man's heart sets him free
forever from all merely human bonds constitutes the
dynamic core of all progressive thought.

In the name of that same God, Moses called for the destruction of the Canaanites. The danger that the Jews
might be infected by heathen religions was only too acute.
The Jews failed to follow this commandment, so it is not
to be wondered at then that they succumbed so often to
the disease.

Joshua's appointment as Moses's successor involved the
risk that the Mosaic revolution might take a "bonapartist"
turn. But Joshua had limited objectives. The war lord of
the Mosaic revolution, unlike Napoleon, harbored no am-
bitions that were in conflict with the revolutionary goal.

He did not turn toward a secondary pharaonism—nor did he let himself be crowned as Napoleon had. The Mosaic ideology was far too powerful within him: Joshua was "full of the spirit of wisdom, for Moses had laid hands upon him" (Deuteronomy 34:9). It is the spirit that drives history onward, the spirit of Pentecost when the holy spirit entered into the souls of the Apostles. Moses's hands had touched Joshua with the sacrament of confirmation.

As we study the history of the Jews, we read of ever new directions from the Lord. The matter is not difficult to understand. This tiny nation was grappling with enormous difficulties. It was not protected by an Atlantic Ocean or a vast land mass—those two tremendous advantages that allowed the American revolution to establish a republic with relatively little hindrance and almost total safety from abroad. Nor did the Jews possess the huge expanses of the Soviet Union, which, after the interventions of the early post-revolutionary years, was not disturbed again until Hitler's invasion, thus gaining the time in which to gather strength so that it was powerful enough to withstand Hitler's onslaught when it occurred.

Nor did the Jews have revolutionary models to guide them, such as the American revolutionists had in biblical Judaism. This fact must be remembered if we are to understand fully what an overwhelming burden was laid upon the Jews by the command to be different from all other nations, and if we consider the fascination that the older civilizations all around held for the young Jewish nation.

Gideon, like Moses, was called upon to fight for the freedom of the Jews. And just as Moses had suppressed the golden calf, so Gideon overthrew the altar of Baal. Then he struck at the Midianites.

After his victory, a common historical phenomenon made its appearance: a grateful nation pleaded with their

victorious general to accept a crown. The event is evidence
of the great attraction of monarchial rule, and of a certain
weakness in a government by the people.

Plainly, the Jews desired a hereditary monarchy when
they said to Gideon:

> "Rule thou over us, both thou, and thy son, and thy
> son's son also: for thou hast delivered us from the
> hand of Midian."
>
> (Judges 8:22)

Gideon was certainly capable enough to be their king.
He must have had a good deal of self-confidence after his
many victories. It was not weakness that moved him to
refuse the crown, just as Christ was to refuse it later.
Gideon's reply bears witness to his greatness. He not only
rejected monarchy as such but rejected it even though he
himself was to have been king:

> And Gideon said unto them, I will not rule over
> you, neither shall my son rule over you: The Lord
> shall rule over you.
>
> (Judges 8:23)

But Gideon's loyalty to the principles of the Mosaic revolution could not stem the reaction. The nation simply
did not want to carry the burden of freedom any longer.
Even one of Gideon's own sons, Abimelech, was tired of
God's rule. In a typical fascist putsch he seized control.
Wealthy supporters enabled him to muster bands of ruffi-
ans much like the storm troopers of National Socialism,
and to slay his brothers who, like Gideon himself, were
opponents of kingship.

> And they gave him threescore and ten pieces of silver
> out of the house of Ba-al-be-rith, wherewith Abime-
> lech hired vain and light persons, which followed
> him.
> And he went unto his father's house at Ophrah,
> and slew his brethren the sons of Jerubbaal, being

> threescore and ten persons, upon one stone; notwith-
> standing yet Jotham the youngest son of Jerubbaal
> was left; for he hid himself.
>
> And all the men of Shechem gathered together,
> and all the house of Millo, and went, and made
> Abimelech king, by the plain of the pillar that *was*
> in Shechem.
>
> (Judges 9:4–6)

We are indebted to Jotham, Gideon's sole surviving son, for a specimen of political cynicism.

> And when they told *it* to Jotham, he went and stood
> in the top of mount Gerizim, and lifted up his
> voice, and cried, and said unto them, Hearken unto
> me, ye men of Shechem, that God may hearken
> unto you.
>
> (Judges 9:7)

Jotham was as sure as any prophet that God was on his side. He then told the Jews a parable:

> The trees went forth *on a time* to anoint a king over
> them; and they said unto the olive tree, Reign thou
> over us.
>
> But the olive tree said unto them, Should I leave
> my fatness, wherewith by me they honour God and
> man, and go to be promoted over the trees?
>
> And the trees said to the fig tree, Come thou,
> *and* reign over us.
>
> But the fig tree said unto them, Should I forsake
> my sweetness, and my good fruit, and go to be pro-
> moted over the trees?
>
> Then said the trees unto the vine, Come thou,
> *and* reign over us.
>
> And the vine said unto them, Should I leave my
> wine, which cheereth God and man, and go to be
> promoted over the trees?
>
> Then said all the trees unto the bramble, Come
> thou, *and* reign over us.
>
> And the bramble said unto the trees, If in truth
> ye anoint me king over you, *then* come *and* put your
> trust in my shadow: and if not, let fire come out
> of the bramble, and devour the cedars of Lebanon.
>
> (Judges 9:8–15)

The most inferior of trees is willing to rule. Here comes to the fore the ambivalence of the symbol of a thorny vine —which is called in this English translation of the Bible both a thornbush and a bramble. In the context of the Mosaic revolution, the burning thornbush became the vehicle through which God commanded Moses to free his people. But the bramble in the framework of Abimelech's counterrevolution becomes the symbol of the revolt against God.

Jotham goes on:

> Now, therefore, if ye have done truly and sincerely, in that ye have made Abimelech king, and if ye have dealt well with Jerubbaal and his house, and have done unto him according to the deserving of his hands:
>
> (For my father fought for you, and adventured his life far, and delivered you out of the hand of Midian:
>
> And ye are risen up against my father's house this day, and have slain his sons, threescore and ten persons, upon one stone, and have made Abimelech, the son of his maidservant, king over the men of Shechem, because he *is*, your brother;)
>
> If ye then have dealt truly and sincerely with Jerubbaal and with his house this day, *then* rejoice ye in Abimelech, and let him also rejoice in you:
>
> But if not, let fire come out from Abimelech, and devour the men of Shechem, and the house of Millo; and let fire come out from the men of Shechem, and from the house of Millo, and devour Abimelech.
>
> And Jotham ran away, and fled, and went to Beer and dwelt there, for fear of Abimelech his brother.
>
> (Judges 9:16–21)

Abimelech was soon to perish at the hand of a woman, who dropped a millstone on his head from the tower of Thebez and crushed his skull. That woman was a precursor of Judith and of Mary.

After the troubled times of judges followed the secondary pharaonism of kings. But before that, the revolutionary Mosaic spirit had flared up once more in Samuel the prophet. Samuel is worthy to take his place beside such mighty figures as Abraham and Simon Peter. But he must be regarded as a profoundly tragic hero, for he lived to see the triumph of secondary pharaonism among the Jews, and God's dethronement. He foresaw the disaster that secondary pharaonism would visit upon the Jews and the eventual failure of those who opposed his words of caution. But he could no longer stem the tide as Gideon once had. All he did manage was to delay it.

Here we see the essence of what it means to be a prophet. The prophet is concerned entirely with a present course of action. He speaks about the future only to make clear what choices men must make. If they will act this way or that, this or that consequence will inevitably follow. If they do not do such and such a thing, such and such consequence will not ensue. The prophet's gift is this—that his insight into the concatenation of sociopolitical events is deeper than that of other men, deeper in that it is more true and more honest.

Jesus's forewarning, for example, that Jerusalem would be destroyed was probably not too difficult a prophecy to make for someone well aware of the political situation, with all its revolutionary and partisan tensions, and of Rome's power. That prophecy was a warning to the people not to let themselves be carried away by misguided political passions. Though Jesus knew that most would not heed him, he wanted to assure at least the survival of those few who accepted him as the son of God.

But back to Samuel. He was born to a woman, Hannah, who had failed to conceive through many years of marriage, although her husband's other wife had. But in the end, God heard Hannah's prayer. He raised her up, as he

had raised the Jews from slavery. Hannah dedicated her
son to God, and, like Mary later, sang a song of praise and
triumph. Among its lines are the following:

> The bows of the mighty men are broken, and they
> that stumbled are girded with strength.
> They that were full have hired out themselves
> for bread; and they that were hungry ceased: so that
> the barren hath borne seven; and she that hath
> many children is waxed feeble.
> He raiseth up the poor out of the dust, and lifteth
> up the beggar from the dunghill, to set them among
> princes, and to make them inherit the throne of
> glory: for the pillars of the earth are the Lord's, and
> he hath set the world upon them.
>
> (I Samuel 2:4–5, 8)

Surely, Hannah sang in the name of all who are downtrodden—the poor, the weak, the insulted. She also sang
in her own name when she spoke of the needy who are
lifted up. She, barren until now, was with child! And finally, her song was also a paean to her son. This child
would play a mighty role in God's design, in the dynamic
work of the divine spirit:

> So the Philistines were subdued, and they came no
> more into the coast of Israel: and the hand of the
> Lord was against the Philistines all the days of
> Samuel.
>
> (I Samuel 7:13)

When he grew old, Samuel appointed his sons to be
judges. But, being corrupt, they failed.

> Then all the elders of Israel gathered themselves
> together, and came to Samuel unto Ramah,
> And said unto him, Behold, thou art old, and thy
> sons walk not in thy ways: now make us a king to
> judge us like all the nations.
> But the thing displeased Samuel, when they said,
> Give us a king to judge us. And Samuel prayed unto
> the Lord.
>
> (I Samuel 8:4–6)

The people's reactionary yearning for a king deeply troubled the aged Samuel. He saw in it a rejection of their God, a sort of idol worship. But after the failure of his sons, and with his own powers fading, he was driven to seek a solution. In his despair he complained bitterly to the Lord:

> And the Lord said unto Samuel, Hearken unto the voice of the people in all that they say unto thee: for they have not rejected thee, but they have rejected me, that I should not reign over them.
>
> According to all the works which they have done since the day that I brought them up out of Egypt even unto this day, wherewith they have forsaken me, and served other gods, so do they also unto thee.
>
> Now therefore hearken unto their voice: howbeit yet protest solemnly unto them, and shew them the manner of the king that shall reign over them.
>   (I Samuel 8:7–9)

The passage clearly shows how God judged the people's wish for a king. It was a betrayal of their Lord, who had delivered them from Egyptian bondage, a relapse into the pharaonic system—it was, in fact, idolatry. Yet the Lord directed Samuel to grant their wish.

But he also directed Samuel to "solemnly warn them, and show them the ways of the king who shall reign over them." If, at the time when the reactionary wave is rising, the progressive forces warn that the measures will bring ill fortune, those progressive forces are afterward in a position to say "I told you so."

Samuel then took the only position that a judge and a prophet in a time of reaction can take:

> And Samuel told all the words of the Lord unto the people that asked of him a king.
>
> And he said, This will be the manner of the king that shall reign over you: He will take your sons, and appoint them for himself, for his chariots, and to

be his horsemen; and some shall run before his chariots.

And he will appoint him captains over thousands, and captains over fifties; and will set them to ear the ground, and to reap his harvest, and to make his instruments of his chariots.

And he will take your daughters to be confectionaries, and to be cooks, and to be bakers.

And he will take your fields, and your vineyards, and your oliveyards, even the best of them, and give them to his servants.

And he will take the tenth of your seed, and of your vineyards, and to give to his officers, and to his servants.

And he will take your manservants, and your maidservants, and your goodliest young men, and your asses, and put them to his work.

He will take the tenth of your sheep: and ye shall be his servants.

And ye shall cry out in that day because of your king which ye shall have chosen you; and the Lord will not hear you in that day.

(I Samuel 8:10–18)

Samuel's prophecy would come true all too soon. King Solomon would exact chattel services from the Jews.

But the Jews were deaf to Samuel's words of warning:

Nevertheless the people refused to obey the voice of Samuel; and they said, Nay; but we will have a king over us;

That we also may be like all the nations; and that our king may judge us, and go out before us, and fight our battles.

And Samuel heard all the words of the people, and he rehearsed them in the ears of the Lord.

And the Lord said to Samuel, Hearken unto their voice, and make them a king. And Samuel said unto the men of Israel, Go ye every man unto his city.

(I Samuel 8:19–22)

The die was cast. Samuel resolved to give in to the people's wish, and to install a king. Samuel made the best of a bad situation by limiting the royal power so that the king would have to rule according to law, and by setting up safeguards that might make a monarchy bearable. But although he himself, ultimately, anointed Saul, he gave vent once more to his sorrow and irremediable opposition:

> And said unto the children of Israel, Thus saith the Lord God of Israel, I brought up Israel out of Egypt, and delivered you out of the hand of the Egyptians, and out of the hand of all kingdoms, and of them that oppressed you:
> And ye have this day rejected your God, who himself saved you out of all your adversities and your tribulations; and ye have said unto him, Nay, but set a king over us. Now therefore present yourselves before the Lord by your tribes, and by your thousands.
> (I Samuel 10:18–19)

After his great victory over the Ammonites, his first heroic deed after assuming the throne, Saul was firmly entrenched. Samuel laid down his judgeship:

> And Samuel said unto all Israel, Behold, I have hearkened unto your voice in all that ye said unto me, and have made a king over you.
> And now, behold, the king walketh before you.
> (I Samuel 12:1–2)

And Samuel once more reproached the Jews:

> And when ye saw that Nahash the king of the children of Ammon came against you, ye said unto me, Nay; but a king shall reign over us: when the Lord your God *was* your king.
> Now therefore behold the king whom ye have chosen, and whom ye have desired! and, behold, the Lord hath set a king over you.
> If ye will fear the Lord, and serve him, and obey his voice, and not rebel against the commandment of the Lord, then shall both ye and also the king that reigneth over you continue following the Lord your God:
> But if ye will not obey the voice of the Lord, but rebel against the commandment of the Lord, then

shall the hand of the Lord be against you, as it *was* against your fathers.

Now therefore stand and see this great thing, which the Lord will do before your eyes.

Is it not wheat harvest to-day? I will call unto the Lord, and he shall send thunder and rain; that ye may perceive and see that your wickedness *is* great, which ye have done in the sight of the Lord, in asking you a king.

So Samuel called unto the Lord; and the Lord sent thunder and rain that day; and all the people greatly feared the Lord and Samuel.

And all the people said unto Samuel, Pray for thy servants unto the Lord thy God, that we die not: for we have added unto all our sins *this* evil, to ask us a king.

And Samuel said unto the people, Fear not: ye have done all this wickedness: yet turn not aside from following the Lord, but serve the Lord with all your heart;

And turn ye not aside; for *then should ye go* after vain things, which cannot profit nor deliver; for they *are* vain.

For the Lord will not forsake his people for his great name's sake: because it hath pleased the Lord to make you his people.

Moreover as for me, God forbid that I should sin against the Lord in ceasing to pray for you; but I will teach you the good and the right way:

Only fear the Lord, and serve him in truth with all your heart; for consider how great *things* he hath done for you.

But if ye shall still do wickedly, ye shall be consumed, both ye and your king.

(I Samuel 12:12–25)

One can see how Samuel is troubled by nagging thoughts about monarchy among the Jews.

To Saul, Samuel's continuing dislike of monarchy could not have been hidden. The guilt feelings, self-doubt, and fits of depression that Saul suffered from were the natural consequence of Samuel's disapproval. Saul could not yet wield the royal power as freely as David would.

Saul's insecurity must have grown even more severe during the war against the Philistines. There was a moment when he was waiting for Samuel to offer sacrifice. But Samuel was so slow in performing the ceremony that Saul lost his patience and made the sacrificial offering himself. That was all Samuel needed to reject Saul in the name of God:

> And Samuel said to Saul, Thou has done foolishly: thou hast not kept the commandment of the Lord, thy God, which he commanded thee; for now would the Lord have established thy kingdom upon Israel for ever.
> But now thy kingdom shall not continue; the Lord hath sought him a man after his own heart, and the Lord hath commanded him *to be* captain over his people, because thou has not kept *that* which the Lord commanded thee.
> (I Samuel 13:13–14)

Saul waged war nonetheless, and victory attended him in war after war. Finally Samuel directed him to fight against the Amalekites. Saul was, however, to take no prisoners but kill all captives. After defeating the Amalekites, Saul, sparing only the king, "put the people to the sword" and took their livestock as booty. Saul, though king only for a short time, seems to have developed feudalistic fellow-feelings for his royal "brother." Once more Samuel condemned him:

> Because thou hast rejected the word of the Lord, he hath also rejected thee from *being* king.
> (I Samuel 15:23)

It was Samuel himself who now killed the king of the Amalekites.

Weighed down with the burdens of constant warfare, rejected by Samuel, and haunted by his own guilt feelings, Saul was naturally prone to periods of severe depression. In the end, he became the victim of his feelings of guilt.

Much weaker than the impetuous David, Saul gave in to superstitious practices. When he and his army were kept at bay by the Philistines, he visited the Witch of Endor, to conjure up the spirit of Samuel who by then had died. The specter—no doubt a projected image of Saul's self-accusations—promptly foretold Saul's death.

A hero in such a tragic frame of mind was bound to lose the crucial battle. Greviously wounded, Saul killed himself, a victim of the conflict among the Jews between the guilt-laden time of kings that lay ahead and the Mosaic revolution against pharaonism.

After Saul's death, nothing could stop David's victory and the triumph of monarchy. The counterrevolution had won out, though it never quite reverted to its starting point, monarchic rule in the Egyptian manner. The Jewish kings were forced to make concessions and never dared to claim divine status for themselves, though Solomon's temple should probably be considered more a monument to the greater glory of King Solomon than to the greater glory of the Lord. With Solomon, Jewish feudalism quickly reached its peak.

In later ages, the example of David and Solomon was frequently raised by Christian feudal lords, and in particular by the heads of the Holy Roman Empire, to fortify their right to rule with biblical precedent. At the back of the imperial crown, which can be seen in Vienna, images of David and Solomon are carved. Since they were kings, the Holy Roman emperors could present them as the kings they were. A different problem of representation was presented by the carving of Moses and Samuel, Elijah and Christ, the revolutionists and prophets. It is not in the interest of any monarchy to glorify those who are in opposition to the right of kings to rule, so their images were reinterpreted.

Reaching its height with Solomon, the Jewish monarchy

soon began to decline both in power and moral strength. During the reign of King Ahab, Elijah the prophet arose. He deserves our close attention because he appeared side by side with Moses and with Jesus on Mount Tabor in the New Testament account.

The attempts made by Jezebel, Ahab's wife, to destroy all the true prophets in Israel is evidence that they represented a movement in opposition to the monarchy. We are told of Jews who hid the prophets in caves from Jezebel's persecution, and provided them with food and drink. We are probably justified in thinking of them as men in the antipharaonic, Mosaic tradition.

Elijah, too, was finally persecuted, after a confrontation with Ahab and Jezebel. At their meeting, Ahab addressed him:

> Art thou he that troubleth Israel? And he answered,
> I have not troubled Israel; but thou, and thy father's
> house, in that ye have forsaken the commandments
> of the Lord, and thou has followed Baalim.
>   (I Kings 18:17–18)

Elijah now summoned all his remaining strength to fight for the God of the Jews. In a dramatic episode he killed the priests of Baal, Ahab's court prophets. These men were apologists, whose sole function was to lend legitimacy to the higher echelons of the Jewish feudal structure by interpreting all actions as being performed according to Jehovah's wishes.

Jezebel tried to arrest Elijah and to have him killed. The free prophets were in difficulty. But Elijah escaped to Mount Sinai, the very place where the Mosaic revolution had begun (where Moses had received God's command out of the burning thornbush) and where later, in a thunderstorm, he had received the tablets of the new law. This time there was no sound of thunder. God addressed Elijah in a "still small voice":

> And he came thither unto a cave, and lodged there;
> and, behold, the word of the Lord came to him, and
> he said unto him, What doest thou here, Elijah?
>
> And he said, I have been very jealous for the Lord
> God of hosts: for the children of Israel have for-
> saken thy covenant, thrown down thine altars, and
> slain thy prophets with the sword; and I, *even* I
> only, am left; and they seek my life, to take it away.
>
> And he said, Go forth, and stand upon the mount
> before the Lord. And, behold, the Lord passed by,
> and a great and strong wind rent the mountains,
> and brake in pieces the rocks before the Lord; *but*
> the Lord *was* not in the wind: and after the wind an
> earthquake, *but* the Lord was not in the earthquake:
>
> And the Lord said unto him, Go, return on thy
> way to the wilderness of Damascus: and when thou
> comest, anoint Hazael *to be* king over Syria:
>
> And Jehu the son of Nimshi shalt thou anoint *to
> be* king over Israel: and Elisha the son of Shaphat
> of Abelmeholah shalt thou anoint *to be* prophet in
> thy room.
>
> And it shall come to pass, that him that escapeth
> the sword of Hazael shall Jehu slay: and him that
> escapeth from the sword of Jehu shall Elisha slay.
>
> (I Kings 19:9–11, 15–17)

On Mount Sinai, we note, even a still small voice meant
a kind of revolution, though the Lord commanded the
kings be changed rather than monarchy be overthrown.

Elijah, accordingly, resolved to set afoot a resistance
movement. Baal had to be driven out of the land of the
Jews. Soon the occasion presented itself for decisive action:

> And it came to pass after these things, *that* Naboth
> the Jezreelite had a vineyard, which *was* in Jezreel,
> hard by the palace of Ahab King of Samaria.
>
> And Ahab spake unto Naboth, saying, Give me
> thy vineyard, that I may have it for a garden of
> herbs, because it *is* near unto my house: and I will
> give thee for it a better vineyard than it; *or*, if it
> seem good to thee, I will give thee the worth of it
> in money.
>
> And Naboth said to Ahab, The Lord forbid it to

me, that I should give the inheritance of my fathers
unto thee.

And Ahab came into his house heavy and displeased because of the word which Naboth the
Jezreelite had spoken to him: for he had said, I will
not give thee the inheritance of my fathers. And he
laid him down upon his bed, and turned away his
face, and would eat no bread.

But Jezebel his wife came to him, and said unto
him, Why is thy spirit so sad, that thou eatest no
bread?

And he said unto her, Because I spake unto
Naboth the Jezreelite, and said unto him, Give me
thy vineyard for money; or else, if it please thee, I
will give thee *another* vineyard for it; and he answered, I will not give thee my vineyard.

And Jezebel his wife said unto him. Dost thou
now govern the kingdom of Israel? arise, *and* eat
bread, and let thine heart be merry: I will give thee
the vineyard of Naboth the Jezreelite.

So she wrote letters in Ahab's name, and sealed
them with his seal, and sent the letters unto the
elders and to the nobles that *were* in his city, dwell-
ing with Naboth.

And she wrote in the letters, saying, Proclaim a
fast, and set Naboth on high among the people:

And set two men, sons of Belial, before him, to
bear witness against him, saying: Thou didst blaspheme God and the king. And *then* carry him out,
and stone him, that he may die.

And the men of his city, *even* the elders and the
nobles who were the inhabitants in this city, did as
Jezebel had sent unto them, *and* as it *was* written in
the letters which she had sent unto them.

They proclaimed a fast, and set Naboth on high
among the people.

And there came in two men, children of Belial,
and sat before him: and the men of Belial witnessed
against him, *even* against Naboth, in the presence
of the people, saying, Naboth did blaspheme God
and the king. Then they carried him forth out of the
city, and stoned him with stones, that he died.

Then they sent to Jezebel, saying Naboth is
stoned, and is dead.

And it came to pass, when Jezebel heard that

Naboth was stoned, and was dead, that Jezebel said
to Ahab, Arise, take possession of the vineyard of
Naboth the Jezreelite, which he refused to give thee
for money: for Naboth is not alive, but dead.

And it came to pass, when Ahab heard that Naboth was dead, that Ahab rose up to go down to
the vineyard of Naboth the Jezreelite, to take possession of it.

And the word of the Lord came to Elijah the
Tishbite, saying,

Arise, go down to meet Ahab king of Israel, which
is in Samaria: behold, *he* is in the vineyard of
Naboth, whither he is gone down to possess it.

And thou shalt speak unto him, saying, Thus
saith the Lord, Hast thou killed, and also taken
possession? And thou shalt speak unto him, saying,
Thus saith the Lord, In the place where dogs licked
the blood of Naboth shall dogs lick thy blood, even
thine.

And Ahab said to Elijah, Hast thou found me, O
mine enemy? And he answered, I have found thee;
because thou has sold thyself to work evil in the
sight of the Lord.

Behold, I will bring evil upon thee, and will take
away thy posterity. . . .

And of Jezebel also spake the Lord, saying, The
dogs shall eat Jezebel by the wall of Jezreel.

(I Kings 21:1–23)

The tone of Elijah's speech is evidence of the severity
of the conflict. Let us note, however, that Elijah seems
not to have protested the institution of monarchy. What
he was opposing so harshly was the transgressions against
the law of God.

After Ahab's death his son Ahaziah continued the struggle against Elijah.

Once, after suffering a serious injury, Ahaziah sent messengers to Baalzebub, the god of Ekron, to inquire if he
would recover. A violent clash with Elijah ensued:

But the angel of the Lord said to Elijah the Tishbite,
Arise, go up to meet the messengers of the king of
Samaria, and say unto them, *Is it* not because *there*

is not a God in Israel, *that* ye go to inquire of Baalzebub the god of Ekron?

Now therefore thus saith the Lord, Thou shalt not
come down from that bed on which thou art gone
up, but shalt surely die. And Elijah departed.

And when the messengers turned back unto him,
he said unto them, Why are ye now turned back?

And they said unto him, There came a man up to
meet us, and said unto us, Go, turn again unto the
king that sent you, and say unto him, Thus saith the
Lord, *Is it* not because *there is* not a God in Israel,
that thou sendest to inquire of Baalzebub the god
of Ekron? therefore thou shalt not come down from
that bed on which thou are gone up, but shalt surely
die.

And he said unto them, What manner of man
was *he* which came up to meet you, and told you
these words?

And they answered him, *He was* an hairy man,
and girt with a girdle of leather about his loins.
And he said, It *is* Elijah the Tishbite.

Then the king sent unto him a captain of fifty
with his fifty. And he went up to him: and, behold,
he sat on the top of an hill. And he spake unto him,
Thou man of God, the king hath said, Come down.

And Elijah answered and said to the captain of
fifty, If I *be* a man of God, then let fire come down
from heaven, and consume thee and thy fifty. And
there came down fire from heaven, and consumed
him and his fifty.

Again also he sent unto him another captain of
fifty with his fifty. And he answered and said unto
him, O man of God, thus hath the king said, Come
down quickly.

And Elijah answered and said unto them, If I *be*
a man of God, let fire come down from heaven, and
consume thee and thy fifty. And the fire of God
came down from heaven, and consumed him and his
fifty.

And he sent again a captain of the third fifty
with his fifty. And the third captain of fifty went
up, and came and fell on his knees before Elijah,
and besought him, and said unto him, O man of
God, I pray thee, let my life, and the life of these
fifty thy servants, be precious in thy sight.

> Behold, there came fire down from heaven, and burnt up the two captains of the former fifties with their fifties: therefore let my life now be precious in thy sight.
>
> And the angel of the Lord said unto Elijah, Go down with him: be not afraid of him. And he arose, and went down with him unto the king.
>
> And he said unto him, Thus saith the Lord, Forasmuch as thou hast sent messengers to inquire of Baalzebub the god of Ekron, *is it* not because *there is* no God in Israel to inquire of his word? therefore thou shalt not come down off that bed on which thou art gone up, but shall surely die.
>
> So he died according to the word of the Lord which Elijah had spoken.
>
> (II Kings 1:3–17)

Here again, it is a flame that came to protect Elijah and kill the soldiers of the king, the same flame that had blazed in the burning thornbush.

Elijah kept the fire of the burning thornbush alive. His influence was so profound and lasting that a legend arose around his memory. Elijah did not die but was carried up to heaven in a whirlwind, in a fiery chariot drawn by fiery horses. His disciple, the prophet Elisha, whom he recruited in the fields much as Christ was to recruit his disciples later, cried out: "The chariot of Israel, and the horsemen thereof." And thus Elijah vanished.

Elijah did not have the power Moses had. Nor did his moment in history favor him as it had favored Moses. His failure made him akin to Samuel. Both men may be likened to Jesus who was killed. Elijah's life and failure remains a thorn in the flesh that continues to nag guiltily at us. Elijah was unable to prevent the downfall. His resistance movement had some successes, but nothing was permanent.

Yet being shunted aside has its advantages. It compels one to delve deeper into the problem of freedom and slavery, of the relationship among men and between man and

God. For the man who fails in his endeavors needs to reformulate the problem in order to examine it in a wider context.

Jesus used his death as his strongest weapon, turning his defeat into attack. But before this let us look at what happened after Elijah's death. Has it not become typical ever since Elijah that prophets are persecuted?

The internecine struggles among the kings of the Jews were much like those among the Capetians. Not many of the kings died of natural causes. At the same time, the Jews repeatedly succumbed to the fascination of the great civilizations that surrounded them.

The adherents of Judaism did not dare to compete with the surrounding civilizations ideologically. All they did was to defend themselves, much as did modern Catholicism until John XXIII broke out of the Catholic ghetto. He who is on principle defensive must expect to lose terrain to those who wage the offensive. The Jews aimed at no more than holding their own ground as well as possible. They hid their ideology under a bushel. Seeing Moses's revolution as limited to the Jews, they were not aware that it had initiated the triumphal march of Mosaic ideology around the world.

But ideas cannot be held in bonds or limited to one group. Once the British had started to democratize their Isles, democracy would not stay confined within their shores. The people of America rose up and clamored for their own freedoms, and won them in fierce struggle. And once the white Americans had won freedom and equality, it was inevitable that black Americans, too, would insist on them.

For the Jews, too, the hour was bound to come when their ideas had to spread and break through the walls that Israel itself had raised around them. The hour came with Jesus of Nazareth.

IV.

REJECTION UNTO DEATH

Behold, this *child* is set for the fall and rising again
of many in Israel; and for a sign which shall be
spoken against.
> —Simeon, according to Luke (2:34)

Jesus knew . . . that it was better to undermine the
state from within, to form cells of resistance, to win
over the hearts of the state's servants. . . . He was an
innovator in the technique of the coup d'état, in-
ventor of the Fifth Column. . . . He knew that in
this manner he was starting on his way to rule the
world.
> —Paul Augier

To guide our feet into the way of peace.
> —Zacharias, according to Luke (1:79)

1. *Mary, the Unruly One*

And Mary said, My soul doth magnify the Lord,
And my spirit hath rejoiced in God my Saviour.
For he hath regarded the low estate of his handmaiden: for, behold, from henceforth all generations
shall call me blessed.
For he that is mighty hath done to me great
things; and holy is his name.

And his mercy *is* on them that fear him from generation to generation.

He hath shewed strength with his arm; he hath scattered the proud in the imagination of their hearts.

He hath put down the mighty from *their* seats, and exalted them of low degree.

He hath filled the hungry with good things; and the rich he hath sent empty away.

He hath holpen his servant Israel, in remembrance of *his* mercy;

As he spake to our fathers, to Abraham, and to his seed for ever.

—Mary, according to Luke (1:46–55)

The personal names of biblical characters are frequently assumed to contain a description of their bearers. Nor is that true only of people who lived in biblical times. Among other nationalities, the early Germanic peoples, for example, the name a man bears is often descriptive of him.

Certain modern authors, too, ascribe decisive significance to personal names, on psychological grounds. Stekel and Jung, for instance, proposed a theory to account for the fact that Alfred Adler wrote on the urge for power, Freud on the pleasure principle, and Jung on the problems of rebirth.* I myself stand on the side of Stekel in ascribing an autosuggestive effect to personal names. Consequently, a person's character can be influenced by those who give him his name.

The meaning of the name Mary, according to what the etymologists tell us, is uncertain, but the meaning that can best be supported is "the unruly one." This meaning seems rather strange because she is most commonly thought of as in the tradition of gentle Ruth. Most people take it for granted that Mary's reply to the angel—"Behold the handmaiden of the Lord" (Luke 1:38)—expresses

---

* In German, the word *adler* means eagle (power), *freud* means joy or pleasure, and *jung* means young.—Translator.

subservience in every respect. The many representations of
Mary that show her in a gentle and meek attitude reinforce that impression. This style of portraiture developed
in the eighteenth, nineteenth, and early twentieth centuries, and gave rise to representations of Mary that can
only be described as cloying and sentimental. Cecil B. De
Mille's film *King of Kings* offers a striking example of this
tradition: a Mary dressed up and made up like Miss Sham-
poo of 1920 is feeding obviously delighted white doves.

Mary's Magnificat must be compared with the song of
Hannah chanted when she brought her son Samuel to the
priest Eli to "give him to the Lord all the days of his life."
The basic concept so exultantly put forth in the Magnificat
—that God is on the side of the weak whom he tries to
strengthen—is the theme of Hannah's song:

> My heart rejoiceth in the Lord, mine horn is exalted
> in the Lord: my mouth is enlarged over mine ene-
> mies; because I rejoice in thy salvation.
> *There is* none holy as the Lord: for *there is* none
> beside thee: neither is *there* any rock like our God.
> Talk no more so exceeding proudly; let *not* arro-
> gancy come out of your mouth: for the Lord *is*
> a God of knowledge, and by him actions are
> weighed.
> The bows of the mighty men *are* broken, and they
> that stumbled are girded with strength.
> *They that were* full have hired out themselves for
> bread; and *they that were* hungry ceased: so that the
> barren hath borne seven; and she that hath many
> children is waxed feeble.
> The Lord killeth, and maketh alive: he bringeth
> down to the grave, and bringeth up.
> The Lord maketh poor, and maketh rich; he
> bringeth low, and lifteth up.
> He raiseth up the poor out of the dust, *and*
> lifteth up the beggar from the dunghill, to set *them*
> among princes, and to make them inherit the throne
> of glory: for the pillars of the earth *are* the Lord's,
> and he hath set the world upon them.

He will keep the feet of his saints, and the
wicked shall be silent in darkness; for by strength
shall no man prevail.

The adversaries of the Lord shall be broken to
pieces; out of heaven shall be thunder upon them:
the Lord shall judge the ends of the earth; and he
shall give strength unto his king, and exalt the horn
of his anointed.

(I Samuel 2:1–10)

In another way—as an aggressive revolutionist who
espouses the rights of the weak and downtrodden against
the strong and the great—Mary is not only in the tradition
of gentle Ruth but also in the tradition of bloody Judith.
It is enlightening to compare Mary's Magnificat with the
song of Judith after she has killed Holofernes:

"Strike up a song to my God with tambourines;
sing to the Lord with cymbals;
raise a psalm of praise to him;
honour him and invoke his name.
The Lord is a God who stamps out wars;
he has brought me safe from my pursuers
into his camp among his people.
The Assyrian came from the mountains of the north;
his armies came in such myriads
that his troops choked the valleys,
his cavalry covered the hills.
He threatened to set fire to my land,
put my young men to the sword,
dash my infants to the ground,
take my children as booty,
and my maidens as spoil.
The Lord Almighty has thwarted them by a woman's hand.
It was no young man that brought their champion low;
no Titan struck him down,
no tall giant set upon him;
but Judith daughter of Merari disarmed him by the beauty of her
    face.
She put off her widow's weeds
to raise up the afflicted in Israel;
she anointed her face with perfume,
and bound her hair with a headband,

and put on a linen gown to beguile him.
Her sandal entranced his eye,
her beauty took his heart captive;
and the sword cut through his neck.
The Persians shuddered at her daring,
the Medes were daunted by her boldness.
Then my oppressed people shouted in triumph, and the enemy
    were afraid;
my weak ones shouted, and the enemy cowered in fear;
they raised their voices, and the enemy took to flight.
The sons of servant girls ran them through,
wounding them like runaway slaves;
they were destroyed by the army of my Lord.

"I will sing a new hymn to my God.
O Lord, thou art great and glorious,
thou art marvellous in thy strength, invincible.
Let thy whole creation serve thee;
for thou didst speak and all things came to be;
thou didst send out thy spirit and it formed them.
No one can resist thy voice;
mountains and seas are stirred to their depths,
rocks melt like wax at thy presence;
but to those who revere thee
thou dost still show mercy.
For no sacrifice is sufficient to please thee with its fragrance,
and all the fat in the world is not enough for a burnt-offering,
but he who fears the Lord is always great.
Woe to the nations which rise up against my people!
The Lord Almighty will punish them on the day of judgement;
he will consign their bodies to fire and worms;
they will weep in pain for ever."*

The Magnificat, as it is reported in the gospel of Luke, is
eloquent testimony of how fully Mary's role as the Lord's
handmaiden is in harmony with her revolutionary energy,
an energy that has its root deep in the most profound tradition of woman's heroism. One can only truly understand this paradox when one totally discards the ideology

* This song of Judith is quoted from the Aprocrypha in The New
English Bible, Oxford University Press and Cambridge University Press,
1970.

of Christian apologetics inherited from the feudal age. That ideology, in the attempt to give a firm basis to the system of feudalism, derives all authority from the authority of God, and thus reduces and debases Christianity to serve as a cover-up.

Against this ideology stands the thesis that every revolution invokes a suprahuman authority to justify its own attack on human authority. Obedience, accordingly, would not be a Christian virtue.

Actually, there probably is such a thing as a duty to obey. It seems to be indicated in the answer Jesus gave to the Pharisees when they questioned him about taxation, an answer that places the burden of decision about whom to obey upon the individual conscience: "Render therefore unto Caesar the things which be Caesar's, and unto God the things which be God's" (Luke 20:25). When one considers that the caesar was shown on the Roman coins as a god, Jesus's answer was a provocation to rebellion by its denial of the divinity of a caesar. But it was also a command to act conservatively by its recognition of a caesar as a temporal authority. In the historical situation and the religious and political horizon of Mary's way of thinking, the revolutionary aspects clearly had to dominate, for Israel was under foreign rule and foreign military occupation.

It is important in this context to note that David was a hero of freedom, pitting himself against those who were foreigners by nationality and by religion. This remains true even though David lacked the strength of character of Gideon, who resisted the temptation of feudalism. David's own family tradition was bound to strengthen him in his stand for freedom and against foreign rule, a position that itself is rooted deeply in Jewry.

Let us turn now to the Magnificat itself and study its

several components. To begin with, the Magnificat, a song of praise, refers to the impending birth of Jesus. The song sings of the mother's expectations for her child and for its future role in history. It takes for granted that that role will be important.

Besides dealing with the child's future, the Magnificat makes some especially important statements about the mother's role as well. Let us therefore examine, not only Mary's vision of her child, but also her view of herself.

Mary begins by praising God, but soon sings of her own glory:

> My soul doth magnify the Lord,
>   And my spirit hath rejoiced in God my Saviour.
>   For he hath regarded the low estate of his hand-
> maiden: for, behold, from henceforth all generations
> shall call me blessed.

Mary's song is prompted primarily by the fact that God has bowed down to "regard the low estate of his hand-maiden." We are reminded here also of the question of obedience. Who is required to obey more completely than a humble maid? And we may remind ourselves also that in those days woman's social position was incomparably lower than it is today.

Mary is subservient to God and God alone. She did in all probability submit outwardly to Rome's quasi-colonial rule over her people. Whether she did so inwardly becomes extremely doubtful once we become sensitive to the emotions that vibrate in the Magnificat.

The song contains a significant parallel between the relation of God and Mary:

> He hath holpen his servant Israel, in remembrance
> of *his* mercy;
>   As he spake to our fathers,
> to Abraham, and to his seed for ever.

The "handmaiden Mary" and the "servant Israel" correspond to each other. It is typical of God to look down at the lowly and lift them up. Her assertion is valid for both herself and Israel when she sings:

> For he that is mighty hath done to me great things;
> and holy *is* his name.
>   And his mercy *is* on them that fear him from
> generation to generation.

Just as Israel had been chosen, and raised from its Egyptian bondage to a decisive role in history, so Mary had been raised from her low estate and chosen to bear the Messiah.

Not Mary alone but Israel as a whole is the progenitor of the Messiah. But what is the Messiah's function? What has he come to do? This much we can be sure of: Mary expected her son to deliver Israel from oppression. The Messiah will deliver Mary and Israel, and set them free.

Yet these thoughts still fail to do full justice to the Magnificat. The song proceeds from the particular, Mary and Israel, to the general. There is more to it than the exaltation of "those of low degree" and the filling of "the hungry with good things." What is being sung about here is a universal revolution of which Israel's exaltation is merely the prototype. For in her song of praise, Mary sings in the most general terms:

> He hath shewed strength with his arm; he hath
> scattered the proud in the imagination of their
> hearts.
>   He hath put down the mighty from *their* seats,
> and exalted them of low degree.
>   He hath filled the hungry with good things; and
> the rich he hath sent empty away.

Mary, and Israel, are lowly and poor, but God's mighty arm has come to the aid of all those who are lowly and hungry.

And, most significant of all, since the child is the subject of Mary's paean, that child as the Messiah will be the historic force that is to serve as God's instrument in scattering the proud and filling the hungry with good things. He will be the agent to implement God's resolve to overthrow the mighty. Thus Mary's and Israel's motherhood are in themselves a high distinction, as the core and main force of the revolution will be of Mary's making.

This is the so-called left-wing Catholic interpretation of the Magnificat, which has been called the Marseillaise of Christianity. The stress of this interpretation is that the words "mighty," "of low degree," "hungry," "rich," are accepted in their literal meanings. Jesus himself throughout the New Testament used "poor" to mean "poor," that is, as descriptive of people who lack the necessities of life. When he said, "Blessed are the poor in spirit for theirs is the kingdom of Heaven," he was speaking of people who were hardly obtaining sufficient food and shelter.

But conservative and reactionary Catholic exegists denounce this reading as being insufficiently spiritual. As the church early began to accrue wealth, and to convert men of means and power, it found itself in a bind because Jesus had unequivocally condemned wealth. It could have enjoined poverty as a condition of a state of grace and condemned wealth, as Saint Francis was to do later. Short of taking that drastic course, it had to deny that Jesus meant "poor" when he said "poor" and "rich" when he said "rich." It had to assert that the word "rich" in such statements as "It is easier for a camel to go through the eye of a needle than for a rich man to enter into the kingdom of God" was used symbolically—that is, by claiming that "rich" meant, not a man who had abundance of goods, but a man who was overattached to his possessions whatever they amounted to quantitatively.

There is, to be sure, a certain validity in these traditional Catholic interpretations because psychological attributes are present in almost every word that describes the condition of a person. It is true that one who commands great power—the "mighty"—may well be less arrogant, less overbearing, less tyrannical than one who commands a small amount of power.

But the act of brushing aside the literal meanings of these words, and interpreting them *only* symbolically, cannot stand up to scrutiny. Jesus labored primarily for those who are lowly in actual fact, not just for those who are symbolically lowly, for those who are actually poor, not just for those who are symbolically poor.

But before turning to Jesus, let us first talk about John the Baptist.

2. *John the Baptist*

John recognized no duty of obedience to human authority. He owed obedience only to God. The diatribes he hurled at Herod would ultimately lead to his death. Although Herod could muster enough courage to throw this messenger of God into prison, it took a woman's persuasion, that of his daughter Salome, to make him take John's life.

John's birth was, once again, remarkable for its improbability: his mother was by then of advanced age. Thus John's very conception was marked as an act of divine providence, charged with significance and portent. The name John means "God bestows grace."

His father Zacharias, who had been mute for many months, found his voice at his son's birth, and began to utter prophecies, painting a picture of what his son's role in life would be. The picture projects a clear conception of the Messiah's function as thoroughly *political* and *religious* in tenor. The parallels with Mary's Magnificat are unmistakable.

Like Mary, Zacharias began his song by praising God. The God of his song is immediately identified as Israel's God. The entire prophecy (Luke 1:68–79) refers to Israel:

> Blessed *be* the Lord God of Israel, for he hath visited and redeemed his people.

The song will praise rapturously the great deeds God will do for Israel. And he will do them in a very special way, working through Zacharias's son John, whose birth is the occasion for the prophecy. God has visited his people by John's birth. But what does that birth signify? What is to be the child's mission? What are God's plans for him? God has

> raised up an horn of salvation for us in the house of his servant David.

The reference to David should be noted: we recall that David gained his throne by his victory over the Philistines.

And now the prophecy proper follows. What are God's plans for John?

> That we should be saved from our enemies, and from the hand of all that hate us.

"All who hate us"—that means all those who have oppressed the Jews, from the Egyptians to the Babylonians, to the Romans who are now occupying Israel. Zacharias, clearly, expects liberation from the Roman yoke.

> To perform the mercy *promised* to our fathers, and to remember his holy covenant;
>   The oath which he sware to our father Abraham,
>   That he would grant unto us, that we being delivered out of the hand of our enemies might serve him without fear,
>   In holiness and righteousness before him, all the days of our life.

Like Mary, Zacharias alluded to Abraham's covenant. But Zacharias was specific in describing the role he foresaw for his son in history's march toward freedom:

> And thou, child, shalt be called the prophet of the Highest: for thou shalt go before the face of the Lord to prepare his ways;
> To give knowledge of salvation unto his people by the remission of their sins.
> Through the tender mercy of our God. . . .

The part John was to play in the great drama of liberation, though important, was thus not to be the leading part. He will "go before the face of the Lord," the Lord who will perform the crucial deed, that of setting the people free. And Zacharias also said that the Lord is "to give knowledge of salvation unto his people by the remission of their sins." There is no mistaking it: for Zacharias, Israel's liberation and the forgiveness of Israel's sins are closely linked.

Israel's prophets always proclaimed that the destiny of the Jews would be determined by its conduct toward God. (The Greek Solon said much the same thing to his people.) And indeed, at the hour of decision in every revolution throughout history, those who feel the stronger faith in the justice of their cause have always won the day. Accordingly, Israel's liberation had to begin with religious reform if it were to be successful.

Zacharias's prophecy ended, however, with verses that stressed another aspect of high importance to our argument:

> whereby the dayspring from on high hath visited us,
> To give light to them that sit in darkness and *in* the shadow of death, to guide our feet into the way of peace.

That visitation means first of all the birth of John. And the great dawn that is now rising, the coming of salvation, is to give light to *all* those who sit in darkness and in the shadow of death.

The verses indicate that John's coming promised to bring guidance and light to all men. Here a universal promise rings out that carries far beyond Israel's initial liberation. One might almost interpret it as a proclamation of the universal role of the Jews as the people which, itself enlightened, will bring light to others.

If Zacharias's Benedictus starts out on an aggressive note aimed at "our enemies" and "all who hate us," it ends in peace—"to guide our feet into the way of peace."

This prophecy of the impending turning point in history, in which John is to play an important part, thus deals with four important events:

(1) Israel's deliverance from the hands of its enemies,

(2) Israel's deliverance by the Lord who will bring the good news of salvation, and of the forgiveness of sins,

(3) God's visitation of Israel to give light to those who sit in darkness, and

(4) Guidance into the way of peace.

I have dwelt at such length upon Mary's and Zacharias's prophecies because they offer an outline, one might say, of the great plan and purpose of the life of Jesus. Nevertheless, much remains obscure, particularly because the second prophecy refers to Christ only indirectly.

But back to John the Baptist. Luke (1:80) added these terse words after Zacharias's prophecy:

> And the child grew, and waxed strong in spirit, and was in the deserts till the day of his shewing unto Israel.

Further on Luke wrote:

> The word of God came unto John the son of Zacharias in the wilderness.
> And he came into all the country about Jordan,

preaching the baptism of repentance for the remission of sins;

As it is written in the book of the words of Esaias the prophet, saying, The voice of one crying in the wilderness, Prepare ye the way of the Lord, make his paths straight.

Every valley shall be filled, and every mountain and hill shall be brought low; and the crooked shall be made straight, and the rough ways *shall be* made smooth; And all flesh shall see the salvation of God.

(Luke: 3:2–6)

John began his active life with a merciless attack upon the people of Israel in the best prophetic tradition:

Then said he to the multitude that came forth to be baptized of him. O generation of vipers, who hath warned you to flee from the wrath to me?

Bring forth therefore fruits worthy of repentance, and begin not to say within yourselves. We have Abraham to *our* father: for I say unto you, That God is able of these stones to raise up children unto Abraham.

And now also the axe is laid unto the root of the trees: every tree therefore which bringeth not forth good fruit is hewn down, and cast into the fire.

(Luke: 3:7–9)

John's attack was aimed at that secondary feudalism whose adherents prided itself on being descended from Abraham: "God is able," he said, "from these stones to raise up children to Abraham." If Abraham's children did not conduct themselves toward God as they should, God could make Abraham's children from these stones on the ground, and reject them!

The central demand of John's moral imperative, which we find hardly a trace of in Christian moral theology, though Christ made the same demand, was his insistence that man ought to be productive and fruitful. Man is called to produce and create something:

> Every tree therefore which bringeth not forth good
> fruit is hewn down, and cast into the fire.

When the Jews mistook him for the Messiah, whom
they imagined vaguely as a radiant, heroic liberator, he
declared:

> I indeed baptize you with water; but one mightier
> than I cometh, the latchet of whose shoes I am not
> worthy to unloose: he shall baptize you with the
> Holy Ghost and with fire:
> Whose fan *is* in his hand, and he will thoroughly
> purge his floor, and will gather the wheat into his
> garner; but the chaff he will burn with fire un-
> quenchable.
>
> (Luke 3:16–17)

The portrait of the Messiah that John drew for the Jews
is not innocuous. To baptize with fire—that means to
plunge the baptizant into God's spirit, the spirit of history
driving irresistibly onward.

Unmistakably, John spoke in the radical manner of
prophets, who spare no one, not even themselves.

Jesus in his turn described John in terms that can hardly
be excelled in their fierce radical intensity:

> What went ye out into the wilderness for to see?
> A reed shaken with the wind?
> But what went ye out for to see? A man clothed
> in soft raiment? Behold, they which are gorgeously
> apparelled, and live delicately, are in kings' courts.
> But what went ye out to see? A prophet? Yea,
> I say unto you, and much more than a prophet.
> This is *he*, of whom it is written, Behold, I send
> my messenger before thy face, which shall prepare
> thy way before thee.
> For I say unto you, Among those that are born
> of women there is not a greater prophet than John
> the Baptist: but he that is least in the kingdom
> of God is greater than he.
>
> (Luke 7:24–28)

John, then, was no conformist and no opportunist. In all he was and did, he showed himself radically opposed to the establishment of his time. And that establishment was to bring about his downfall.

Mark tells us of John:

> And John was clothed with camel's hair, and with a girdle of a skin about his loins; and he did eat locusts and wild honey.
>
> (Mark 1:6)

Such ascetic dress and conduct serve several purposes. John's attire, for one thing, proclaimed a return to Israel's heroic age, their long march, their years of wandering. For another, John had reduced to a minimum his need of those things that the Marxists call man's "economic basis," thereby gaining freedom from economic chains. A man who can subsist on locusts and wild honey need not be afraid that his employer will withhold his wages. In order to be as free as possible to build the "superstructure" of his being, John reduced his "basis" to the barest essentials.

Jesus identified John with Elijah. This recognition not only does John the most extraordinary honor but, conversely, is a sign of high esteem for Elijah:

> But I say unto you, That Elias is come already, and they knew him not, but have done unto him whatsoever they listed. Likewise shall also the Son of man suffer of them.
>
> Then the disciples understood that he spake unto them of John the Baptist.
>
> (Matthew 17:12–13)

This radical ascetic John himself defines his relation to Jesus as follows:

> I *am* the voice of one crying in the wilderness, Make straight the way of the Lord.
>
> (John 1:23)

Or, in the theological language of the gospel according to John:

> There was a man sent from God, whose *name* was John.
> The same came for a witness, to bear witness of the Light, that all men through him might believe.
>
> (John 1:6–7)

And John the Baptist himself, who lacked the slightest ambition to outshine Jesus, said:

> this my joy therefore is fulfilled.
> He must increase, but I *must* decrease.
>
> (John 3:29–30)

Yet even John, weakened by long imprisonment, asked of Jesus in an attack of doubt:

> Art thou he that should come? or look we for another?
>
> (Luke 7:19)

But Jesus sent in answer the tremendous news:

> Go your way, and tell John what things ye have seen and heard; how that the blind see, the lame walk, the lepers are cleansed, the deaf hear, the dead are raised, to the poor the gospel is preached.
>   And blessed is *he*, whosoever shall not be offended in me.
>
> (Luke 7:22–23)

In Jotham's tale about the bramble that was willing to accept kingship, the thornbush, once the symbol of God's command to Moses to offer heroic resistance to the pharaoh, is turned into the symbol of royal power gained by lawless means. Just so, Judith's heroic and patriotic deed of cutting off Holofernes's head is reversed when Salome, Herodias's daughter, demands the head of John, because he has defied Herod and Herodias. The death of Holofernes freed Judith's people from their enemy and oppressor; John the Baptist was killed in the interest of the oppressors of the people. When Holofernes was killed a usurper was destroyed; when John the Baptist was killed, a liberator, a revolutionist, a prophet, was lost to the world. In his defiance one sees the connection with Elijah, who had challenged his king, Ahab, and his king's wife, Jezebel:

> For Herod himself had sent forth and laid hold upon John, and bound him in prison for Herodias's sake, . his brother Philip's wife: for he had married her.
>
> For John had said unto Herod, It is not lawful for thee to have thy brother's wife.
>
> Therefore Herodias had a quarrel against him, and would have killed him; but she could not:
>
> For Herod feared John, knowing that he was a just man and an holy, and observed him; and when he heard him, he did many things, and heard him gladly.
>
> And when a convenient day was come, that Herod on his birthday made a supper to his lords, high captains, and chief *estates* of Galilee;
>
> And when the daughter of the said Herodias came in, and danced, and pleased Herod and them that sat with him, the king said unto the damsel, Ask of me whatsoever thou wilt, and I will give *it* thee.
>
> And he sware unto her, Whatsoever thou shalt ask of me, I will give *it* thee, unto the half of my kingdom.
>
> And she went forth, and said unto her mother, What shall I ask? And she said, The head of John the Baptist.
>
> And she came in straightway with haste unto the king, and asked, saying, I will that thou give me by and by in a charger the head of John the Baptist.
>
> And the king was exceeding sorry; *yet* for his oath's sake, and for their sakes which sat with him, he would not reject her.
>
> And immediately the king sent an executioner, and commanded his head to be brought: and he went and beheaded him in the prison.
>
> And brought his head in a charger, and gave it to the damsel: and the damsel gave it to her mother.
>
> (Mark 6:17–28)

The life of John the Baptist is a blood-stained drama of heroic resistance. He himself knew that he was a precursor, preparing men for the events that would immediately follow. John urged a radical return to God—that is, he asked men to turn their backs upon the world. He baptized to cleanse men of the blemishes of their impurity; and he preached fruitfulness, the good fruit that each man must bear.

3. *Jesus*

This book focuses on Moses and Jesus because our theme is the relation between the Judeo-Christian tradition and revolution. As for Jesus, whose life and work invite a psychological analysis, our problem is more complex.

As to the political aspects of the problem, I propose the following theses:

(1) Jesus was conscious that he was continuing in the tradition of Abraham, Moses, Samuel, Elijah, and John the Baptist. He fully accepted what those men had accomplished.

(2) Jesus wanted to continue working in the spirit of these men, but did not cling slavishly to the letter of the law.

(3) Jesus wanted to give greater depth to the basic idea of Judaism, and render it universal.

(4) To achieve the universal revolution, Jesus regarded the Jews as the "elite," the vanguard. They were predestined for this task by their history and should have become the primary carriers of the Christian dynamic.

(5) Jesus's main concern was to reconcile mankind with God the Father.

(6) Jesus's political goal was a universal society based

on the fundamental principle of universal brotherhood, a society that would recognize different functions of members of society but reject all differences of caste or class.

(7) He wished to establish the criterion that the sincerity of Christian endeavor was to be exhausted by its ethically grounded creativity, just as John the Baptist had claimed.

(8) Jesus was thwarted by the resistance of the Jewish establishment, and resolved to lay down his life in supreme proof of his sincerity.

(9) He established a small Jewish community whose task it was to prepare the way for the victory of God's spirit—the dynamic force in history—in order ultimately to realize a human society of universal brotherhood under one Father.

(10) Because the majority of the Jews was not willing to follow him, he resigned himself to taking a roundabout way, a detour.

(11) If universal brotherhood becomes a reality, then there cannot any longer be any enslavement or persecution of any people and so not of the Jews.

(12) Just how universal brotherhood is to be organized when it is attained remains undefined in detail, precisely because that organization will have to differ according to the different economic and technological conditions in each given time and place. The universal principle of brotherhood has to be worked out in ever changing forms at every new technical level.

(13) A world of universal brotherhood, once established, will also be a world of peace.

These theses are fully in harmony with the prophecies of Mary and of Zacharias. They coincide with Mary's Magnificat in that they imply the downfall of the mighty and the rich because universal brotherhood is incompatible with either the feudal or the capitalist system. And

they agree with Zacharias that Israel's salvation, the forgiveness of sins, universal enlightenment, and ultimately
the way to peace, are rooted in the teachings of Jesus.

A point we must be quite clear about is Jesus's attitude
toward the Jewish liberation movement and Palestine's
occupation by the superpower Rome. It must have been
obvious to any man of political judgment that a rebellion
against the Roman armed might had no chance of success.
Jesus, accordingly, foretold the fall of Jerusalem and the
catastrophic failure of the Jewish revolt:

> And when ye shall see Jerusalem compassed with
> armies, then know that the desolution thereof is
> nigh.
>   Then let them which are in Judaea flee to the
> mountains; and let them which are in the midst of it
> depart out; and let not them that are in the coun-
> tries enter thereinto.
>   For these be the days of vengeance, that all things
> which are written may be fulfilled.
>   But woe unto them that are with child, and to
> them that give suck, in those days! for there shall be
> great distress in the land, and wrath upon this
> people.
>   And they shall fall by the edge of the sword,
> and shall be led away captive into all nations: and
> Jerusalem shall be trodden down of the Gentiles,
> until the times of the Gentiles be fulfilled.
>   (Luke 21:20–24)

Jesus, of course, did not advocate that Palestine remain
a Roman possession, but he thought it necessary that
Rome's military resources be recognized as a fact. For the
one and only realistic road to Jewish liberation led through
Rome. If Rome could be converted to universal brotherhood, it would necessarily abandon imperialistic policies
because imperialism is incongruent with brotherhood. If
this could be brought about, the Jews, and not only they,
would be freed of the yoke of foreign domination. Rome,
therefore, had to be conquered ideologically from within.

And indeed, Peter and Paul were soon to concentrate their missionary efforts on Rome.

It would be a mistake, however, to assume that Jesus was aiming at the liberation of the Jews alone. The principles of brotherhood had to be disseminated throughout the nations of the world: "Go into all the world and teach the gospel to the whole creation" (Mark 16:15).

As Jesus was expanding his objectives and giving them a universal foundation, he was also deepening their religious dimension. Moses limited his immediate objectives to the Jewish nation, though he did not exclude the idea that the God of the Jews was the God of all mankind. But Jesus proclaimed that all men on earth are God's children, thus laying the foundation of the universal brotherhood of man. Jesus's aim was to alter radically the very structure of man's basic religious consciousness. That alteration would inevitably bring about far-reaching sociological changes and, ultimately, changes in political structures.

For purposes of comparison, we might take a look at the liberalizing tendencies now at work in the eastern-bloc nations. The "reduction of the cult of personality"—the official term for destalinization—at first produced only a loosening of controls in various ways, such as increased freedom of speech. Changes in the political structure occur much more slowly.

Similarly, Jesus was aiming first of all at changing men's religious consciousness, but the changes he sought were so profound that they were bound to lead in time to decisive political changes. Thus Christ's self-set task was much more far-reaching than that of Moses. He could have carried it out completely only if he had had Israel's full support right from the start. But that was not to be.

Jesus, then, was faced with the problem of revolution. His opponents were Jerusalem's Judaic priesthood of the time, which under Roman occupation maintained relations with the Roman governor that were of a somewhat dubious character.

The reactionary Jewish priesthood of the day, totally lacking in dynamism, was the victim of a kind of compulsive neurosis, a religious fanaticism that constricted the horizon of religious reality. Thus the command to keep the Sabbath holy, for example, was translated into a set of rigid rules. In order to resist the overpowering attractions of the rich and mighty civilizations of their time, the Jews had isolated themselves from the cultures around them. Actually they had withdrawn into a voluntary ghetto.

The problem, then, was this: Would the Jews, spread over a wide area, yet persisting in their hopeless, ideologically defensive attitude, be able to reach out to new horizons? Could either the whole nation or at least a large part of it do so? Jesus faced this question from the start. His fearless attacks, imbued with an aggressiveness so characteristic of prophets, were directed against a sector of the Jewish priesthood. He expressed himself in a language so radical, so sharp, that it left nothing to the imagination. We have heard such language once before, from John the Baptist. Jesus's prophetic aggressiveness, however, was clearly inspired by love for his people, the Jewish people whom he wanted to arouse. This combination of love and aggression is the distinctive mark of prophetic criticism.

Jesus's direct attack on Jewish orthodoxy is ablaze with the fire of the burning thornbush. And his criticism culminated in the mightiest challenge that could be hurled at Jewish orthodoxy. He told the Jewish high court that he would come upon God's cloud to judge all men, even the judges of the court themselves. At this point Jesus was already inviting death, but he desired that all Israel should follow him up to that crossroads. His prophetic language was "extreme," "excessive," "discourteous," and "immoderate." Shall we compare it with the diplomatic niceties of the decretals issuing from the Holy See? Jesus spoke of "reeds in the wind," "luxurious garments," "the courts of kings." Here are a few examples of his plain talk:

> Give not that which is holy unto the dogs, neither cast ye your pearls before swine, lest they trample them under their feet, and turn again and rend you.
>
> (Matthew 7:6)

The people listened to him:

> And it came to pass, when Jesus had ended these sayings, the people were astonished at his doctrine:
> For he taught them as *one* having authority, and not as the scribes.
>
> (Matthew 7:28–29)

He dealt radically with those who were to follow him:

> And another of his disciples said unto him, Lord suffer me first to go and bury my father.
> But Jesus said unto him, Follow me; and let the dead bury their dead."
>
> (Matthew 8:21–22)

Or take his curse upon the unrepentant towns:

> Woe unto thee, Chorazin! woe unto thee, Bethsaida! for if the mighty works, which were done in you, had been done in Tyre and Sidon, they would have repented long ago in sackcloth and ashes.
> But I say unto you, It shall be more tolerable for Tyre and Sidon at the day of judgment, than for you.
> And thou, Capernaum, which art exalted unto heaven, shalt be brought down to hell: for if the mighty works, which have been done in thee, had been done in Sodom, it would have remained until this day.
> But I say unto you, That it shall be more tolerable for the land of Sodom in the day of judgment, than for thee.
>
> (Matthew 11:21–24)

Not to be forgotten are his terrible assaults upon the scribes and Pharisees:

Woe unto you, scribes and Pharisees, hypocrites! for ye pay tithe of mint and anise and cummin, and have omitted the weightier *matters* of the law, judgment, mercy, and faith: these ought ye to have done, and not to leave the other undone.

Ye blind guides, which strain at a gnat, and swallow a camel.

Woe unto you, scribes and Pharisees, hypocrites! for ye make clean the outside of the cup and of the platter, but within they are full of extortion and excess.

Thou blind Pharisee, cleanse first that *which is* within the cup and platter, that the outside of them may be clean also.

Woe unto you, scribes and Pharisees, hypocrites! for ye are like unto whited sepulchres, which indeed appear beautiful outward, but are within full of dead *men's* bones, and of all uncleanness.

Even so ye also outwardly appear righteous unto men, but within ye are full of hypocrisy and iniquity.

Woe unto you, scribes and Pharisees, hypocrites! because ye build the tombs of the prophets, and garnish the sepulchres of the righteous.

And say, if we had been in the days of our fathers, we would not have been partakers with them in the blood of the prophets.

Wherefore ye be witnesses unto yourselves, that ye are the children of them which killed the prophets.

Fill ye up then the measure of your fathers.

Ye serpents, *ye* generation of vipers, how can ye escape the damnation of hell?

Wherefore, behold, I send unto you prophets, and wise men, and scribes: and *some* of them ye shall kill and crucify; and *some* of them shall ye scourge in your synagogues, and persecute *them* from city to city:

That upon you may come all the righteous blood shed upon the earth, from the blood of righteous Abel unto the blood of Zacharias son of Barachias, whom ye slew between the temple and the altar.

Verily, I say unto you, All these things shall come upon this generation.

(Matthew 23:23–36),

These sentences should be remembered by those naive antisemites who believe they would not have killed Jesus as the Jews of Jerusalem had done. His thesis has a particularly sophisticated psychological logic, which prefigures elements of importance that depth psychology has pinpointed. Whoever states self-assuredly and self-righteously that he never killed a prophet who told him unpleasant truths has never examined himself honestly. He has never tried to illuminate the dark abysses of his inner being, filled with his resentments, death wishes, evilness. Therefore, because of such unsuspected depths, he may well be overcome by his own evil at the decisive moment. But one who is self-critically aware of the evil tendencies in himself that have to be carefully controlled will shy away from voicing moral indignation at a "criminal." He will remind himself that under certain social and psychological conditions he might act just as the despised others are acting. Given this orientation he is much less likely to kill a prophet when attacked by him. Since he knows himself, he will evaluate the validity of the accusations, meanwhile keeping his hostile reactions under better control.

Even those who fully accept Jesus's message must admit, in fairness to the Jewish conservatives (including Judas), that no leadership of any nation would listen to such verbal assaults without conceiving the idea that the trouble-maker must be silenced.

Jesus's idea of the kingdom of God, a thoroughly Jewish idea of theocracy, is only secondarily a political idea. Jesus's primary concern is man's relation to God; and the kingdom of God is ultimately "not of this world" but world-transcending. Yet a kingdom that is not of this world may still be "for this world."

Especially significant for all future times is Jesus's principle of fruitfulness, or, to use a modern term, productivity. His principle of universal brotherhood is probably

even more explosive. Both principles are largely hidden
under a bushel basket by the official church.

Let us deal first with productivity. The extraordinary
importance of this principle stems from the fact that the
increase of a society's productivity makes the realization
of universal brotherhood immeasurably easier. It could be
said that fruitfulness is first of all a religious principle:
greater fruitfulness is a sign of a more loving relation to
God. But productivity is *also* worldly: to translate love of
neighbor into a living reality, material goods must be produced and made available. The more we produce, the more
we can give to our neighbor.

In the Bible the basic symbols of fruitfulness are very
concrete things. First among them is the fig tree. In view
of the principle's extreme importance, we should look
closely at decisive passages. Earlier I mentioned John the
Baptist's words of the "fruits of true conversion," and his
warning that "every tree which bringeth not forth good
fruit is hewn down, and cast into the fire." (Matthew
3:10)

According to Jesus, fruitfulness is the mark of the genuine and true prophet:

> Beware of false prophets, which come to you in
> sheep's clothing, but inwardly they are ravening
> wolves.
>   Ye shall know them by their fruits. Do men gather
> grapes of thorns, or figs of thistles?
>   Even so every good tree bringeth forth good fruit;
> but a corrupt tree bringeth forth evil fruit.
>   A good tree cannot bring forth evil fruit, neither
> *can* a corrupt tree bring forth good fruit.
>   Every tree that bringeth not forth good fruit is
> hewn down, and cast into the fire.
>   Wherefore by their fruits ye shall know them.
>   (Matthew 7:15–20)

In a characteristically prophetic gesture, Jesus puts a
curse on a barren fig tree:

Now in the morning as he returned into the city,
he hungered.

And when he saw a fig tree in the way, he came
to it, and found nothing thereon, but leaves only,
and said unto it, Let no fruit grow on thee hence-
forward for ever. And presently the fig tree withered
away.

(Matthew 21:18–19)

The parable of a barren fig tree served Jesus as a means
of presenting God's mercy:

He spake also this parable; A certain man had a
fig tree planted in his vineyard; and he came and
sought fruit thereon, and found none.

Then said he unto the dresser of his vineyard,
Behold these three years I come seeking fruit on this
fig tree, and find none: cut it down; why cumbereth
it the ground?

And he answering said unto him, Lord, let it alone
this year also, till I shall dig about it, and dung it:

And if it bear fruit, well: and if not, *then* after
that thou shalt cut it down.

(Luke 13:6–9)

The mustard seed and its growth are compared with the
kingdom of God:

Then said he, Unto what is the kingdom of God
like? and whereunto shall I resemble it?

It is like a grain of mustard seed, which a man
took, and cast into his garden; and it grew, and
waxed a great tree; and the fowls of the air lodged
in the branches of it.

(Luke 13:18–19)

There is the famous parable of the sower:

A sower went out to sow his seed: and as he sowed,
some fell by the way side; and it was trodden down,
and the fowls of the air devoured it.

And some fell upon a rock; and as soon as it was
sprung up, it withered away, because it lacked
moisture.

And some fell among thorns; and the thorns
sprang up with it, and choked it.

> And other fell on good ground, and sprang up,
> and bare fruit an hundredfold.
>
> (Luke 8:5–8)

But surely the most important parable for a Christian work ethics is that of the master who entrusted talents to his servants:

> For *the kingdom of heaven is* as a man travelling into a far country, *who* called his own servants, and delivered unto them his goods.
>
> And unto one he gave five talents, to another two, and to another one; to every man according to his several ability; and straightway took his journey.
>
> Then he that had received the five talents went and traded with the same, and made *them* other five talents.
>
> And likewise he that *had received two*, he also gained other two.
>
> But he that had received one went and digged in the earth, and hid his lord's money.
>
> After a long time the lord of those servants cometh, and reckoneth with them.
>
> And so he that had received five talents came and brought other five talents, saying Lord, thou deliveredst unto me five talents: behold I have gained beside them five talents more.
>
> His lord said unto him, Well done, *thou* good and faithful servant: thou has been faithful over a few things, I will make thee ruler over many things: enter thou into the joy of thy lord.
>
> He also that had received two talents came and said, Lord, thou deliveredst unto me two talents: behold, I have gained two other talents beside them.
>
> His lord said unto him, Well done, good and faithful servant; thou hast been faithful over a few things, I will make thee ruler over many things: enter thou into the joy of thy lord.
>
> Then he which had received the one talent came and said, Lord, I knew thee that thou art an hard man, reaping where thou hast not sown, and gathering where thou hast not strawed:
>
> And I was afraid, and went and hid thy talent in the earth: lo, *there* thou hast *that is* thine.

His lord answered and said unto him, Thou
wicked and slothful servant, thou knewest that I reap
where I sowed not, and gather where I have not
strawed:
Thou oughtest therefore to have put my money to
the exchangers, and *then* at my coming I should
have received mine own with usury.
Take therefore the talent from him, and give it
unto him which hath ten talents.
For unto every one that hath shall be given, and
he shall have abundance: but from him that hath
not shall be taken away even that which he hath.
And cast ye the unprofitable servant into outer
darkness: there shall be weeping and gnashing of
teeth.

(Matthew 25:14–30)

It is of course true that all these parables carry a spiritual message. The talents in the above parable are usually
interpreted as the word of God, which the cautious servant refused to spread. But the proof that Jesus's earnest
concern was religious lies precisely in his commitment to
the social realities. The self-isolation of the desert monks
is an aberration, though it, too, may be of relevance to the
human community.

Let us note, then, how definitively Jesus opposes and
condemns unfruitfulness. Let us note also how much he
emphasizes that we must take risks. It is after all true, as
the timorous servant in the parable points out, that every
investment represents a risk. But such risks must be accepted, because there can be no productivity without them.
Jesus urged us to leave our fears behind and invites us
to take chances.

Though the category of fruitfulness means little to
Christian moral theologians, it was of such importance to
Jesus that he sought fruitfulness even in his own death:

Verily, verily, I say unto you, Except a corn of wheat
fall into the ground and die, it abideth alone: but if
it die, it bringeth forth much fruit.

(John 12:24)

Nothing could illustrate more strikingly how very much in earnest Jesus was in his conception of God's kingdom than the fact that he included even his own death in his thoughts on fruitfulness. If he could not convince men by his life, he would convince them by his death.

Let us consider another of his principles, which is also of the highest social significance—the principle of brotherhood. The brotherhood of man rests on religious foundations. Because God is the father of all men, all men are brothers and ought to love one another. Because they are brothers they must help one another to be fruitful.

That God is the universal father is so is quite independent of our being aware of him as a universal father. Jesus's injunction to his apostles, to "go into all the world and teach the whole creation" does of course mean that all men should become conscious of God as the father of all. A life led in full awareness that we are God's children and each other's brothers is radically different from a life led in denial of this elementary fact. Yet such a denial does not alter the existential truth.

"Souls there are many; but there is not a single one among them with whom I am not in communication through that sacred core within it, which is expressed by the Our Father," Paul Claudel wrote. To achieve universal brotherhood, the community of Christians is meant to function as an elite, in that it has the responsibility to serve as a prototype of how this brotherhood is to be practiced. It should be the nucleus from which a light radiates into the world. Membership in the brotherhood of Christians is wide open to all men.

Brotherhood is to be extended to all men, of course. But it is best put to the test when it requires a special effort to put it into practice. This means in our relations with those who are, literally or figuratively, dirty. These are the heathen, the publicans, the people who do the dirty physical labor, criminals, prostitutes, and the like; the sick, the poor, the hungry, and those in prison; the fools, the simpletons, the losers.

This is why Jesus was particularly concerned with the unfortunate. Once again, his language is as radical as can be:

> And he shall set the sheep on his right hand, but the goats on the left.
>
> Then shall the King say unto them on his right hand, Come, ye blessed of my Father, inherit the kingdom prepared for you from the foundation of the world:
>
> For I was an hungered, and ye gave me meat: I was thirsty, and ye gave me drink: I was a stranger, and ye took me in:
>
> Naked, and ye clothed me: I was sick, and ye visited me: I was in prison, and ye came unto me.
>
> Then shall the righteous answer him, saying, Lord, when saw we thee an hungered, and fed thee? or thirsty, and gave *thee* drink?
>
> When saw we thee a stranger, and took *thee* in? or naked, and clothed *thee*?
>
> Or when saw we thee sick, or in prison, and came unto thee?
>
> And the King shall answer and say unto them, Verily I say unto you, Inasmuch as ye have done *it* unto one of the least of these my brethren, ye have done *it* unto me.
>
> Then shall he say also unto them on the left hand, Depart from me, ye cursed, into everlasting fire, prepared for the devil and his angels:
>
> For I was an hungered, and ye gave me no meat: I was thirsty, and ye gave me no drink:
>
> I was a stranger, and ye took me not in: naked, and ye clothed me not: sick, and in prison, and ye visited me not.
>
> Then shall they also answer him, saying, Lord, when saw we thee an hungered, or athirst, or a stranger, or naked, or sick, or in prison, and did not minister unto thee?
>
> Then shall he answer them, saying, Verily I say

unto you, Inasmuch as ye did *it* not to one of the
least of these, ye did *it* not to me.

(Matthew 25:33–45)

The passage calls for *caritas*, the first and most immediate assistance that we must give our neighbors. But it
would be a mistake to believe that *caritas* is all that is required. The church has cause to regret its failure to develop
strategies that would be fundamentally brotherly. It has
made little attempt to go beyond alms-giving, that is, of
succoring the needy. The day-to-day techniques of waging
the battle against hunger, which advanced nations are developing via science, are most emphatically the concern of
Christianity. Christ himself, teaching within the confines of the social and economic structure of Rome, could
only lay down the basic principles. He could not demand
the development of agricultural machinery or the establishment of a world health organization, such as contem-
porary social forms make possible. But modern Christianity can, and therefore must, do so.

The detailed plan by which universal brotherhood is to
be realized will vary, obviously, with the given level of
productivity. Advances in science and technology, and advances in mass education, may contribute to making the
brotherhood of man a living reality.

Just as the fatherhood of God has its own symbols, so
has brotherhood, as will be shown. When Jesus saw that
the conservative, or more precisely, the reactionary forces
among the Jewish religious and political leadership were
too strong for him, and that the vast majority of the people
were concerned only with life from one day to the next
and with their own affairs, he sacrificed his own life, thus
endowing his tenets with a dynamism that could not fail
to carry conviction. He came into Jerusalem peacefully,
riding on a donkey. He came to meet his death. He had
selected the first day of Passover as the day of his death.

Jesus here consciously linked his action to the tradition of Abraham and Moses. The ram the Lord had sent to Abraham was killed to set Israel free for God; the paschal lambs had died in the dark Egyptian night in place of Israel's first-born; the first-born of the Egyptians had died for Israel's freedom. Just so, Jesus would die so that his people could free themselves from the elements of Judaism that threatened to diminish the divine spirit.

At the seder Jesus attended the night before his crucifixion, the meal that was to become known in the Christian world as the last supper, Jesus established the central symbol of human brotherhood: the eucharist. On a subconscious level the sharing of food and drink implies the sharing of the same mother. The shared meal is thus the rite establishing or confirming brotherhood, as the rituals of a number of peoples make clear. At this seder (celebrated without a lamb, it seems) the main fare was unleavened bread, the food of the Jews in the desert, and wine. Christ identified himself with bread and wine, thus creating, as it were, the core of universal brotherhood.

If there is anything that expresses fully the essence of universal brotherhood, it was this Passover supper in Jerusalem. It was that Passover supper that linked the glorious Jewish past with a significant present and a future rich in vistas.

Becoming one with Jesus was conceived of as the core of the Christian life. It remains to this day the heart of Christianity, despite all those antibrotherly tendencies that pervade the liturgy. There is no greater symbol of brotherhood than the eucharist, although this point is made all too rarely in the textbooks of Christian theology.

What, then, are the ethical and moral imperatives that Christianity imposes on revolutionary movements? Although Jesus is always on the side of the lower classes of society in their upward striving, these classes are nonetheless bound to deal humanely with the upper strata opposing them. For example, if the bourgeoisie seizes the power in a feudal state, it must not put the members of the old aristocracy to death. (It was, however, unavoidable for Moses, for example, to kill the Jewish reactionaries at Mount Sinai.) And the victors of a successful revolution have no right to liquidate the former ruling class. Rather, the new society should provide positions that enable the exponents of the old order to contribute to the new society because everything that is fruitful and productive should be encouraged.

A group that partakes together of the eucharist is unequivocally egalitarian. The quality of being united in brotherhood with Jesus is far more important than any of intellectual, social, or other differences among men. The principle of brotherhood does not imply the notion of a specific economic system. But it seems clear that a classless and casteless society is most congenial to the principle.

However much specific characteristics are lacking, any Christian society based on the principle of brotherhood must be inherently antihierarchic. The practice of electing functionaries is more in accordance with the principle of equality than that of staffing privileged positions in society by virtue of birth. The feudal system is always characterized by gaps between the upper and the lower strata that correspond more closely to the distance in a father-child relationship than to the span in a fraternal one.

It hardly has to be pointed out that the socialist society as envisioned by the Marxist, that is, one in which the private ownership of the means of production has been eliminated, is a closer expression of the principles of brotherhood than is the capitalistic society, where the ownership of the means of production as well as the enormous income differences create basic inequities in the distribution of power and responsibility. The early Christian communities believed that only community property was in line with Christian principles. They, and later on Thomas More, went further than the later Marxists, who at the beginning intended to make only the means of production, not consumer products, communal property. So far as the system of ownership is concerned, the Jesuits in Paraguay have championed communal ownership of everything.

At this writing there is no country that has achieved a successful lasting union between the bourgeois-democratic principle of freedom, whose essence lies in the idea of freedom of opinion, thoughts, and conscience, with the socialist-communist democracy of ownership. Maybe this will come about through Christian example.

We know that Jesus went to his death with open eyes. He left us as his legacy the eucharist, which we are to share in memory of him.

By his death, Jesus proclaimed his commitment to universal brotherhood with absolute moral seriousness. He provoked his death by his claim that would brook no contradiction, that he was God's own son and the ultimate judge of the world. The Jewish high court could not very well put itself under the jurisdiction of the accused, which would indeed have been unheard of, but condemned him to die. It was a death that bore fruit a hundredfold.

The Jewish leaders, as we know, turned Jesus over to Pilate, whom they could readily control. A former partisan of Sejanus, Pilate at that time found himself in an awkward position vis-à-vis the emperor Tiberius. Sejanus had been selected by Tiberius to be his coregent. A passionate antisemite, he planned a "final solution of the Jewish problem" much like that of Hitler. During one of Tiberius's absences, Sejanus made preparations for a coup-d'état to make himself sole ruler. Tiberius found him out in time, and had him executed. A "de-Sejanization" followed, a purge in which a number of leading Romans lost their lives. Pilate managed to survive somehow. Quite likely, the Jewish leaders were in possession of information that made him vulnerable to blackmail. Not daring to acquit Jesus against their wishes, Pilate ordered the inscription "King of the Jews" to be placed on the cross as a symbolic substitute for an acquittal.

And so Jesus died a slave's death (in those days people from higher social ranks were executed by beheading) in irrefutable proof of the earnestness of his commitment.

Karl Marx's view, based on the social conditions of the early capitalist era, that "religion is the opium of the people," may have been true for his own time because religion was then so misused. But it is invalid with regard to the founder of Christianity or his first Christian community. A man who lets himself be killed for universal brotherhood can hardly be accused of wanting his legacy to be "the opium of the people."

On this note let us close this chapter about Jesus Christ. It may appear inconclusive because in Jesus's life the revolutionary element did not relate to social issues with the same relevance as it did in the life of Moses. Jesus's whole personality was revolutionary; his aims were universal, all-embracing. But his revolutionary energy was primarily channeled into religion. The political implications of his teaching would emerge only in the long run. To this day they are far from being realized. In Christ's own time and social setting, it was possible to conceive the idea of universal brotherhood, but it was impossible to make that brotherhood a reality. Moses had a more limited, preliminary goal, which was within his reach. But Jesus's goal was long-range. For it to be achieved, a community had first to be established. That community was founded on Christ's death, and on the death of the Christian martyrs.

V.

THE DETOURS OF THE HOLY SPIRIT

> But, Lord, it is not easy to escape you—and if he
> does not approach you in his radiance, then let
> him do it in his darkness, and if he cannot come
> by the straight way, let him come by crooked
> ways. . . .
>
> —*The Satin Slipper*, Paul Claudel

JESUS'S DEMAND that he be recognized as the son of God
put the Jewish high court in a position of such extreme
difficulty that it is unlikely that any organization of the
establishment, in any age, would have been able to meet
such a situation. Objectively, we must recognize that the
high court slowed down the course of history. It is guilty
of resisting the spirit of history that had expressed itself
through Moses, the prophets, and Jesus. Had history's
course run straight, there would have been a Jewish people led by Jesus, who started to bring about a messianic
revolutionary transformation of the earth that would lead
to the universal brotherhood of man.

Originally, the target of Jesus's endeavor was Jerusalem
and its environs. That region, however, was inhabited by
a much more conservative and tradition-bound population than that of the north. It was in this region that

Jesus met his death. Judas Iscariot was a native of this central region. To Judas, law and order meant infinitely more than they did to Peter and John, for example, who came from the north near Lake Genezareth. Apparently Jesus's teachings and his personality initially made a great impression on the inherently conservative Judas. But his unresolved inner conflict compelled him to act out his need for conservatism, and he betrayed Jesus. He regretted this so deeply after Jesus's death that he hanged himself.

But Jesus soon had to accept the fact that those who would carry on his teachings were the Jews of Galilee, up on the northern borders, rather than the Jews of central Judaea. He recruited his best disciples from among the socially restless border regions of Palestine whose inhabitants were receptive to dynamic, revolutionary ideas. His tactics demonstrate that he tried to conquer the core of the Jewish nation through mobilizing the people of the border regions. And the people in the border regions, obviously, were in much closer contact with neighboring pagan nations.

Let us get ahead of our argument for a moment by comparing the situation in which Jesus worked with the situation in the present-day Catholic church. Stated roundly, the dynamism of the church today is to be found in its fringe groups. To look for dynamism in today's Rome is virtually pointless. And the explanation does not lie in the Italian national character, as anti-Italian forces would have us believe. If Italians are less dynamic than others in ecclesiastical matters it is simply because of their geographical closeness to Rome.

The progress of the holy spirit follows certain laws. If allowed to take its course undeterred, the sequence would have been: from Moses to Jesus to the Jews. Or, more precisely, from Moses to Jesus to the core of the Jews.

But very soon Jesus realized he would have to take a

detour with the Jewish people: he would have to work through the border regions to the core of the Jews to the kingdom of God.

Jesus, that is, tried to penetrate to the center by a flanking movement, after recruiting his elite troops from the border regions. His initial attempt, to win over the Jews of Jerusalem, which would mean winning over most of the Jews, had failed. After that failure, he selected from among the Jews of the border regions a group of men who were to carry his message into the future. His intention was that Jews were to be the nucleus of the society of the future. After the Jews had accepted him, they were to address themselves to the pagan nations beyond the borders of Palestine. But then he realized that the church of the future would have to have its beginnings among people from the border regions of Palestine and its pagan neighbors.

This strategy is of great importance. It illustrates typical response of the holy spirit to any attempts at squelching it—which is to take a roundabout way. Hegel's expression, "the cunning of reason," aptly describes the matter. But, and this is extremely important, Jesus's detour does not mean that the main direction was abandoned. The demand made on the Jewish core, that it assume the responsibility of leading the world to new heights, that demand remained unchanged. As Paul saw, God's spirit never frees any group from performing its allotted task. The detour, which is nothing other than a temporary expedient whose inadequacy is obvious, can never be considered as a performance of the task. Christian self-awareness would be wholly different from what it is today if Christians had a profound consciousness of belonging to a continuum of Abraham, Moses, and Elijah that leads to John the Baptist and Jesus and Peter.

A metaphor of the holy spirit's progress as I conceive of

it might be the course of running water. Water, when blocked in its course, seeks a way around the obstacle—a detour. Wellspring, stream, and river are all traditional symbols of the holy spirit. Jesus himself speaks to the Samaritan woman of "living waters." And Dostoevsky, referring to the Book of Revelation, uses the image of the river for the "seeking of God":

> Reason and science have always, today and from the very beginning of time, played a secondary and a subordinate part; and so they will to the end of time. Peoples are formed and moved by quite a different force, a force that dominates and exercises its authority over them, the provenance of which, however, is unknown and inexplicable. That force is the force of an unquenchable desire to go on to the end and, at the same time, to deny the existence of an end. It is the force of an incessant and persistent affirmation of its existence and a denial of death. It is the spirit of life, as the Scripture says, "rivers of living water," the running dry of which is threatened in Revelation. It is the aesthetic principle, as the philosophers call it, and ethical principal, with which they identify it, the "seeking of God," as I call it much more simply.

Thus I am in good company when I use water as a metaphor for the holy spirit.

The main point I want to make is to call attention to the way water acts when its course is impeded by obstacles. After the detour made necessary by the obstacle, water—and the holy spirit—still reaches the same goal. Nietzsche may have had something similar in mind when he praised the greatness of those who are willing to make temporary deflections.

> Great men and streams go crooked ways,
> yet reach their goal.
> This is the greatest courage:
> They do not fear crooked ways.

But let us return to the community of Jews from the Palestinian border regions and of converted pagans that constituted the early Christians. Without idealizing this early church, no one doubts that its initial dynamism was extremely strong. At first it was entirely religious in orientation. To be sure, it contained a variety of diverging conceptions, and schisms and heresies were not slow to arrive.

We all know that the Roman Catholic church eventually succumbed to that same conservative timidity and traditionalism that had imbued the Jewish establishment. It, too, had a tendency to extinguish and block the holy spirit.

This direction can be seen in the great schism, which was the secession of the Eastern Orthodox church from the Roman church in 1054.

The doctrinal differences between Roman Catholics and the schismatics (the Eastern Orthodox church and, in some ways, the Anglican church) are negligible. The nearest thing to a true difference is the distinction between the "honorary chairmanship of the bishop of Rome" (Eastern Orthodox church) and the "jurisdictional primacy of the Pope" (Roman Catholic church). The principal issue, however, is not so much this matter of jurisdictional primacy as the psychological attitudes that reveal themselves through such titles. In actual fact, an Eastern bishop would have objected little to Rome's jurisdictional primacy, if only the popes had treated bishops with less arrogance. Centralism of the sort that celebrated its most recent triumphs under Pope Pius XII is exactly the kind of thing that will prevent the Eastern patriarchs from ever acknowledging the Pope of Rome as the true center of the church. Pius XII voiced a principle that inhibited initiative among the bishops: "I do not want collaborators, I want executives to carry out my decisions." The lower officials in the Roman Curia treated the bishops accordingly: bishops were kept standing before the officials' desks while making their reports about their dioceses.

Despotic centralism inhibits the creative life of the holy spirit. A schism became necessary to preserve and assert the vital selfhood of the apostolate, if the holy spirit was to do his work. Just as the converted pagans served the Jews as their progressive avantgarde, so the schismatics later on performed that function for the Roman church.

To summarize then, the schismatics took a stand against the usurpation of power by Rome and in defense of the autonomy of the eleven apostles against the twelfth. And even though the schism doubtless went too far, the blame for it must very largely be laid to Roman centralism. In what way other than secession could the bishops defend their independence so long as Rome would not accept any attitude short of slavish subservience? Thus the schismatics, in their unremitting advocacy of episcopal autonomy, were the defenders of a basic Christian value.

The movement for episcopal autonomy within the Roman church burst forth vehemently at the Second Vatican Council. In response to the pressures of its rebellious, democratizing members, Rome agreed to take measures to reduce centralism and the jurisdiction of the apostle of Rome (the pope) and agreed that bishops would be allowed more authentic power.

If we concede that the existence of the schismatic churches had an influence in the decentralization of the power of the Church of Rome, it follows that Roman Catholic bishops should be grateful to the schismatics, who had taken upon themselves the trials of conscience and the burden of the schism, and had provided that the holy spirit could operate freely in this matter. While Rome, the center of Roman Catholicism, long resisted the truth that there were twelve apostles rather than just one, the schismatics maintained the right of the other eleven against the one at Rome.

If reconciliation is to come about, which is a possibility only if the schismatics accept a well-defined jurisdictional primacy for Rome, and Rome in turn accepts a well-articulated autonomy for the bishops, Rome's contribution would be to establish Peter as the vicar of God and the bishops' contributions would be apostolic autonomy. But the process must be reciprocal. The mere "submission" of the schismatics, returning, like prodigal sons, into the arms of a forgiving Roman father would do no good. A like exchange will some day be required at the incomparably more difficult meeting between Judaism and Christianity.

Let us pause a moment to recapitulate. The fact that the Jewish establishment refused to make itself accessible to the current of the holy spirit, thus forcing the holy spirit to seek a detour, does not mean that the holy spirit had wholly forsaken the Jews. It continued to trouble them, and again and again they proved themselves capable of flashes of true spirit and revolutionary ardor. These flashes were more apt to occur at the periphery of Jewish society than at its center.

Catholicism has had its effects upon the Jews. When the Jews adopted monogamy, they probably did so because of Catholic influence, though they could have accepted it more directly from the Jew Jesus.

Within Roman Catholicism, the situation is similar. Under the influence of the schismatics, Rome discovered the individual and autonomous importance of the bishops. If the Roman church had had the "right spirit," it would not have needed the schismatics to lead them to that discovery.

And what holds true of the schismatics also holds true

of the heretics—"our alienated brethren" as we now call them and could just as well have called them in the past.

Let us look at one example of so-called heresy. A traveler in Czechoslovakia will notice many church steeples crowned by a chalice. These are Hussite churches. Hussites are the followers of John Huss, who initiated what was considered a heretical movement in fourteenth-century Bohemia. Among his teachings he advocated that laymen as well as priests drink the communion wine. An admirer of Wycliffe, Huss was burned at the stake for heresy. The Hussites' insistence that the laity share in the wine of the eucharist undoubtedly sprang from a genuine feeling of Christian brotherhood. The Second Vatican Council reexamined the question of the laity drinking the eucharist wine and did not find it antithetical to church dogma. The Hussites, it would seem, had preserved authentic Christian concerns that Rome had suppressed. The Hussites' insistence that the laity partake of the eucharist wine reveals that the laity was esteemed much more highly among the sectarians than in Rome. In that matter then, the holy spirit was active among the Hussites, not in Rome.

Be that as it may, however, the effort to extirpate the Hussites with fire and sword was criminal. An attempt should have been made to utilize their special revolutionary ardor in the service of all Christendom.

One definition of heresy may then be that it is the reflection of orthodoxy's extreme mistakes.

So-called heretics, then, like schismatics, are in possession of certain precious truths that they could add to the treasure of the church.

The significance of the fact that now the eucharist in both species is accessible to the layman, at least under certain conditions, a privilege previously reserved to the ordained clergy, is that the layman, since the Second Vatican

Council, is being held in higher esteem in the eyes of the
church, though he is far from being fully reenfranchised.
Since the days of the early church, the layman was practically without rights in his church. Pius XII defined him
as Aristotle defined the slave—"an instrument in the hands
of the master." This is an example of a typical detour
that the holy spirit is forced to make when existing circumstances block his path.

Let us note, then, that even within Catholicism the holy
spirit is active primarily on the periphery and is reflected
in actions that sometimes poise close to heresy. At the
center, the holy spirit's work is exceedingly difficult. This
ponderous slow-moving center should, however, be looked
at fairly. Let the schismatics and heretics put themselves
in Rome's place. It is not only much simpler to leave
things as they are. Even more to the point is the fact that
those who are responsible for many souls must necessarily
be much more careful to avoid mistakes than those responsible for just a few. I myself readily admit that a free-
wheeling intellectual has it much easier than an official of
a church responsible for millions. This, though it ought to
keep us from passing harsh judgment on the individuals
involved, does not relieve us of our duty to say aloud what
we believe to be the truth.

I should also point out here that the schismatics did not
acquit themselves any better than did Catholic orthodoxy
with regard to a good many of the matters they raised. The
Greek church, for example, was just as blind as Rome in
its attitude toward biblical exegeses put forth by Protes-
tants. The schismatics, then, have valid reason to empha-
size the fact that they stood for genuine Christian values,
but they are not free of failures that they share with Rome.

Except for some sectarian groups (such as the Method-
ists) or individual priests, pastors, and lay people who
fifty years after their time will serve as a convenient alibi

amid universal failure, it must be said that all groups within the Judeo-Christian tradition are alike in making common cause with feudalism and with capitalism.

Because of this, the holy spirit has sometimes had to take a roundabout way through atheism. Prior to the French revolution, the Christian churches identified themselves almost completely with a feudal system that was largely indifferent to the rights of the individual conscience. The union between "throne and altar," whose very mention is distasteful today to apologists of the church, seemed to belong to church dogma. It was a fundamental mistake of the church.

The American and the French revolutions fought for and won freedom of press and of inquiry. As Christians, we ought to consider a country a good country if Jesus could work unimpeded in it. And it seems undeniable that he would encounter fewer difficulties in the United States of America than in a country pervaded by the influence of the church.

Now, if the principle of universal brotherhood is neglected by the church, ("church," in the sense of ecclesiastical hierarchy); if the feudal patriarchate reigns unimpeded within the church; and if the church raises enormous obstacles to the solution of universal problems—then the holy spirit has to go outside Christianity.

Christian brotherhood movements have long existed in the form of the mendicant orders. In contrast with the chivalric orders that have not yet been dissolved, the mendicant monks represent the principle of universal brotherhood, and thus are surely among the most Christlike of Catholic orders. These elements *within* the church —though once again peripheral and at the point of being heretical—offered the church the most intense form of Christianity. But the hierarchy at the center, unwilling to practice liberty or equality or fraternity, refused the gift. Again the holy spirit had to take a detour. This time he took the route of anti-Christian ideologies.

Anyone looking objectively at the international situation today can easily see that liberalism within the church, such as has prevailed since John XXIII, would not have been possible without the American and French revolutions, or without that of Garibaldi's. That the index of forbidden books was finally dropped was due in part to conscious (American) Christianity, and in part to the unconscious, anticlerical "Christianity" of the protagonists of the French revolution and of the freemason Garibaldi. One should then keep in mind that it was these revolutionists who forced the church to acknowledge the demands of the individual conscience.

Nor should we speak ill of Marxism. It is clear that the mendicant orders translated the ideal of poverty into a living reality. It is no accident that nothing in Christianity impressed Lenin more profoundly than Francis of Assisi. The mendicant orders in the church are the forerunners of communism. The history of these Christian mendicants and of their restoration to a place of honor will provide the subject matter for many thoughtful books. These mendicants gave the church its typical alibi for decades to come. And when the church did at last recall that universal brotherhood meant concern and responsibility for the poor, the sick, and the old, it owed a substantial part of its reawakening largely to free-thinking socialists and communists. Without the American liberals and the Marxist socialists, the liberals and socialists within the church would have had little success in effecting official change.

Colonialism, an inglorious chapter in the history of Christian love of neighbor, fell into disrepute after 1945. The Roman Catholic church, which had been the handmaiden of colonialism, even though no sanction for it can be found in the teachings of Christ, is indebted to the two superpowers for finally becoming anticolonialist. A few exceptional priests are now called upon by the Roman church as evidence of past anticolonialism. (One of these is Bartolomé de Las Casas, the fifteenth-century Spanish missionary and historian who devoted his life to bettering the plight of the exploited and oppressed New World Indians.) The United States of America, itself a former colony, as well as the Soviet Union now oppose colonialism. Under the pressure of the superpowers, the United States and the Soviet Union (their own well-known interests are not relevant here), and under the pressure of anticolonial movements in the colonies themselves, the Catholic hierarchy accepted the necessity of decolonization. Not only did they hurriedly develop indigenous clergy in the newly emerging nations but they also appointed a number of black bishops and cardinals. Paul assumed the role of spokesman for these nations in his encyclical Populorum Progressio.

In this way, non-Catholics help Catholics to become more Catholic. This should be admitted. Nothing disarms the adversary more completely than the admission that we have learned something from them. Nothing is more "undiplomatic" than the attempt to force the other party to capitulate. Jesus, who was blameless, could demand this— but not the church, which is laden with guilt.

We thus are brought to the realization that non-Christian ideologies became the guardian of the fire of the burning thornbush when the official church was trying to stifle that fire. The holy spirit took his most daring detour when it detoured through areligious ideologies.

The holy spirit does not know cowardice. In spite of the tradition of papal infallibility, John XXIII dared to say plainly that a recognition of one's own defects and limitations is necessary for all. Only this recognition can provide the foundation of universal community. Acknowledgment by liberals and Marxists of their Judeo-Christian origins can only be achieved by Christianity's admitting that it betrayed its own principles.

Neither the schismatics and heretics nor Orthodox Jews are in a more comfortable position vis-à-vis the ideal of universal brotherhood than is the Catholic church. None of them can exclude themselves from the community of guilt.

As we all know well, in this world of imperfect men, neither side in a controversy will ever be completely in the right. If we are not prepared to grant to others, with utter sincerity, the merits of their position, all communication becomes empty. Men who can make peace only on the condition of the complete surrender of the other side are unrealistic.

How does the great peace come about? Zacharias expressed it when he said: "To guide our feet into the way of peace."

All things must be gathered home.

This leads me to recall a personal experience. A well-known professor of Catholic dogmatics came to me and asked me to "act as progressively as possible" in theological matters because, he said, "we theologians are so bogged down in scholasticism that only the lay theologians can rescue us." For the truly earnest among the Roman Catholic clergy, the last great detour that still remains possible is dissenting and working for a Catholic, supranational Christianity. Only such a Christian can still advocate liberalism and social conscience because he alone enjoys a jester's license.

At the election of John XXIII, the holy spirit succeeded via a kind of Freudian slip—the cardinals meant to elect a "transitional pope." And so they did—but in a sense other than they intended. This is a typical detour of the holy spirit.

VI.

CHURCH AND REVOLUTION

A new mysticism rises in the red sky, and gathers as its followers all those who were the first in Jesus's days to be taught and won over by him—the oppressed, the exploited, the humble, the sinners, the slaves. . . . To adopt the powerful image of a Slavic writer, every time the church neglects a trust, someone arises by God's strange decree to gather that truth up again and present it to the church at sword's point: this is what the Marxists are doing today with their doctrine of the working man's emancipation, and of the International.

—Paul Augier

The atheist is he who searches for a purer God.

—Lagenau

CHRISTIANITY was early to exhibit the symptoms of ambivalence toward political revolution. This stemmed from the circumstance that Jesus had concentrated all his efforts on religious revolution; political revolution was to follow later. In order to establish a new world order, Jesus had to create first of all a new morality. It would have made no sense for him to get involved in the quarrels of a moribund society if the entire principle of how a new society should be constructed was still unformulated.

For Moses, the basis of society was man's relation to a just God. For Jesus, then, the basis of society was the *new* relation of man to God. Only after the religious foundation had been firmly established, only then could a new and lasting society structured on the principle of universal brotherhood come into being. And the Christian principle of brotherhood was certain to ignite one revolution after another.

Jesus's concentration on the religious, the fact that his concern with political matters was merely incidental, were factors that partially explain why religious and political action did not proceed abreast. But we must attend also to a second consideration.

For a time Jesus seemed to have believed that the end of the world was imminent. This misapprehension explains a number of things, among which was the slightness of Jesus's concern with the institution of marriage. If we expect the world to end in a year or two, there is no point in trying to reform the world. The castaway on a desert island, a Robinson Crusoe, convinced that he has ten or so days to live, will make do with the most primitive things and conditions. Luther's defiant statement, "If I knew that I was to die tomorrow, I would still plant a tree today!," is not the stand that all would take.

One more point. The church Jesus wished to have erected had one purpose: to proclaim the gospel. Its primary concern was man's relation to God.

I should pause here to clarify what I mean by the word church. If the church is to mean the totality of believers, that is, of all its members, these members have to fulfill the most diverse social functions. These members working in a variety of fields will (also in good conscience) react differently in the same or similar situations. The church will have no influence on their attitudes or conducts unless strictly religious questions (for example, restrictions of religious freedom) are involved.

The concrete, sociologically definable church, as August M. Knoll rightly observes, is embodied in the power of its hierarchy, in its authority to command because of its institutions and jurisdictions. And just as Jesus de facto recognized the laws of Rome, so the church recognized the established power structure even while being aware of its defects.

The church, being a clerical hierarchy, does not feel committed to any social system. At best, it can mitigate the iniquities produced by a social system, but it never tries to go any further. The church does not insist on changes in the principles of the social system. As Knoll has demonstrated, the church is so totally opportunistic in its relation to society that it will recognize any de facto system.

Its opportunism arises from two sources. For one thing, the church must be able to act, which means that it generally must have at least a minimum of toleration for its existence from the state. Second, the church is interested in its secular expansion, its economic, power-political, and prestige interests, for whose benefit its social theories are promptly adapted. Knoll's remark that "the church's concept of property at any given time is an apologia for the possession of what the church owns at that given time" is therefore quite true. It is just about unimaginable that a natural-law theologian in an official ecclesiastical position would come to the conclusion that this or that church property might be unlawfully held.

E. K. Winter and August M. Knoll have explained in their writings the process by which the adaptation of the church to new revolutionary movements is brought about.

Let us then break down the pattern between church and state into six phases.

PHASE ONE. The church in this concrete sense, is at first either tolerated or harassed, by the state (social system X, based on ideology X) in which it establishes itself. For as long as it finds itself in this situation, it settles for being allowed to exist and is prepared to promise in return that it will not subvert the society by revolutionary changes.

PHASE TWO. When the church expands sufficiently, the state becomes willing not just to tolerate it but to assure it of a large measure of acceptance. This is what happened, for instance, under Constantine. Even the ruler himself may then become a Christian.

At this point in its career the church lapses into a hardly avoidable corruption. Its dignitaries are rising in social status and are obtaining high rank in society, high in secular terms as well as in church hierarchy. In consequence they grow accustomed to enjoying the advantages of the upper classes; and they now "discover" that the establishment is "Christian." The ideology of the system, they now see, is really in full harmony with Christian unity. In other words, a system based on non-Christian ideas is now whitewashed with Christian paint, and therefore also serves the economic interests and the desire for prestige and power of the clergy, especially that of the higher clergy. At the same time the higher clergy adopts the manners and the demeanor of the members of the upper levels of society. In phase two then, the church is a pillar of the state, lending quasi-divine authority to the governmental process.

During phase two other groups shift their position. After the church links with the power structure, certain groups, such as the pagans after Constantine's time, are tolerated or rejected, and—these are bitter words—sometimes driven outside the law.

At the same time, ascending classes come into conflict with system X. They make large new demands and no longer accept the legal bases of the existing system. In phase two then, the lower groups become increasingly virulent and disturb the serenity of the upper strata.

PHASE THREE.   The church, now in alliance with the system, assuming increasingly the role of the system's defender, opposes attacks from below as "un-Christian." System X, now whitewashed with its new coat of Christianity, is regarded as the ideal of the Christian social structure. During phase three, agitators for social system Y (which will be dominant in phase four) arise among the oppressed groups and tangle with the church and its "natural law," a principle serving almost no interests but that of the church.

PHASE FOUR.   Now the cycle has come full turn. The social group with ideology Y has wrested control from the old establishment, from the upholders of the old ideology, with its recent Christian coat of paint. At this point the church is out of power again.

PHASE FIVE.   This parallels the situation in phase two and phase three. The learned interpreters of the natural law are now providing a Christian gloss for ideology Y, as they had done for ideology X. They discover axioms in the natural law that supply Christian support for the prerogatives of the new establishment. The new establishment of social system Y welcomes such assistance with an eagerness that is all the greater in proportion to the pressure being exerted by the new lower strata (embracing anti-Christian ideology Z) on the rise. Once more the ecclesiastical hierarchy attains a position among the establishment.

PHASE SIX.   This is a repetition of phases one and four.

Anti-Christian ideology Z has provided the underpinnings of social structure Z, and the church is outside, biding its time until it again unites with the establishment.

Knoll's insights need to be supplemented by additional consideration. Indeed, he himself has presented some of them in recent lectures, although these have not yet been published.

If we understand the church as the mystical body of Christ, it embraces all Christians, and perhaps even all men of goodwill. Yet there are always some men representing revolutionary ideas who have no place within the official church hierarchy. In greater or lesser opposition to the church hierarchy, they are frequently subjected to repressive measures. Nonetheless, in a mystical sense they belong to the church, and within the church they are the true bearers of the holy spirit. They are the Christian guardians of the flames of the burning thornbush.

The fate of such groups of men typically evolves as follows: While the church hierarchy is accommodating itself to the power structure of social system X, scattered small groups emerge who feel it insufficient that the iniquities inflicted on the lower strata are being mitigated. These groups demand a fundamental transformation of the system, or even the establishment of a new system upon new foundations.

Such groups may disagree, for instance, with Paul's dictum "Masters, be good masters, and servants, be good servants!" (a statement that must be understood in the light of Paul's expectation of the world's end). Instead they hold with Moses, and their war cries are "Away from Egypt's bondage!" and "No more pharaoh!" Away with slavery, away with overlords. A nation of brothers has no place for slavery. There is no point here in raising the common defense for societies based on inequality, that is,

that many slaveholders behave much better than many a
high official in a society based on equality and brotherhood. This argument, though true, is beside the point. A
vast difference lies between a society resting on immoral
foundations, in which some admirable people rise above
the society's basic immorality, and a society based on
moral foundations, which contains immoral individuals
who violate its principles. Needless to say, the ideal is a
moral society peopled by moral individuals.

The left-wing Christian, the dissenter, demands the
fundamental transformation of the system, and does so on
Christian grounds. He thus finds himself in an extremely
complex situation. He is at odds with the secular system-
supporter as well as with the ecclesiastical system-supporter. In the eyes of the former (assuming he considers
himself Christian) he is a dangerous radical who, in
the name of Christianity, "undermines the structure of
human civilization." The system-supporter cannot imagine
any structure different from his own.

The ecclesiastical system-supporter, on the other hand,
counters the dissenter's Christian arguments with the reminder that "all worldly rule is forever imperfect." Slavery, he asserts, must be accepted as a consequence of
original sin. He draws on similar rhetoric to cover other
matters. He denies the dissenter's right to speak in the
name of Jesus or of the prophets or of the holy spirit,
because the dissenter is not part of the "teaching church"
but only of the "lay church." Some of the ecclesiastical
system-supporters may nonetheless be shaken in their
naive faith in the absolute rightness of the church's
structure by the arguments of the dissenters.

He helps the dissenter with one hand while hindering
him with the other. The bad conscience of the establishment does its part to prevent or at least delay decisive
counterrevolutionary action.

To the extent that the clerical system-supporters are part of the establishment, the dissenter's prophetic impulse must turn against them as well as against the secular leaders though it attacks them only in their secular role. When the rebellious peasants rose up against the archbishop of Salzburg, who was also the temporal ruler of Salzburg, he excommunicated them. As a successor of the apostles, who should have taken an antifeudal position, he acted inappropriately. These peasants were rising not against the successor of Paul the tentmaker or John the fisherman but against a feudal lord living in luxury. The Lollards' cry—

> When Adam delved and Eve span
> Who was then the gentleman?

—carried a thoroughly Christian message.

The dissenters within the church most often carry Christian "dynamite" (as Knoll calls it in his lectures) that they introduce into the society even while the system-supporters preach appeasement. The feeling among the "noble Romans" that Christianity was plebeian and that its doctrine of universal brotherhood undermined the very foundations of Roman civilization, was in this sense fully justified. Champions of the elitarian principle, and in this sense reactionaries, accuse Christianity of subverting the great civilizations. From their point of view they are entirely justified. They are also right in holding Christianity, together with Judaism, responsible for the French, the American, and the Russian revolutions.

It cannot surprise us that a large number of dissenters fail to maintain the prophet's stance of loyalty to the church together with the resistance to the church. The attacks of the prophets upon the leading circles of the Jews were moral appeals to these circles to change their ways; they were not attacks on the substance of Judaism.

But such appeals are usually misunderstood, and the dissenters, who make them, meet with no understanding and are defamed. Persecuted within the church, denied even a hearing, in former days burned at the stake, the dissenters are bound to lose their trust not only in the church's system-supporters who persecuted them but also in the church itself. Once driven to despair of the church, they tend to go to extremes. They leave the church and begin to address their Christian appeal to some other group, such as a religious sect. Nobody has the right to sit in judgment on such men except, possibly, those few men who have managed to maintain their opposition *within* the church, for the church's own sake. The doctrinaire conformists certainly have no right to judge them.

In extreme cases, an entire such group may cut itself off from Christianity, construct its own anti-Christian ideology—and pursue what is basically a thoroughly Christian goal.

More than once in the course of history, prophetic thinkers within the ranks of the church have offered to Christianity progressive social concepts, concepts far ahead of their time. Christian socialist and communist utopias are very much older than Marxism. But the church has never seized such opportunities, and thus the holy spirit was compelled once more to find a detour and to utilize even atheism in order that history might proceed in its course.

Understandably, the dissenters within the church have some contact with those heretics and ideologists outside the church who are striving for analogous social goals. This fact gives them an extremely important function. If the rising revolutionary groups should succeed in gaining control of the society, the formerly defamed dissenters will provide the official church with an initial support in a new order. The teachers of the church's social doctrine now find that the dissenting thinkers have already developed all the religious theory that the new system needs to lend conviction to the new system's ideology.

This addition—the pattern of the role of the dissenter, to the sequence of phases presented above is necessary. Perhaps the addition will make the sequence appear less cynical—but very much sadder. For the men who suffer most in the course of events, the dissenting innovators, the men who are ahead of the times, are precisely those who are most essential to the future of the church.

One point that deserves to be stressed here is that the anti-Christian tenor of the new egalitarian ideologies is largely a reaction against the alliance between the establishment and clerical hierarchy.

This analysis does not cover everything, of course, but is still useful in casting light on essential characteristics of social progress. An honest attempt to present the relation between Christianity and church on the one hand, and revolution on the other, leads us to the following formula, which the present book has tried to prove.

The great revolutionary line of succession runs from Abraham, Moses, Samuel, Elijah, and John the Baptist to Jesus. Jesus regarded religion as primary, politics as secondary. For Moses and for Samuel, religion and politics were still a single, undivided unity. But Christianity, ideologically, is an explosive element that in the long run was bound to undermine the "western" structure of lordly power.

While Christianity, and the lower, seemingly subordinate yet extremely important, sectors of the ecclesiastical structure, are revolutionary, the church (considered as a clerical hierarchy) is conservative and indeed often reactionary. The great revolutionary movements—the American revolution, the French revolution, and communism—represent secularizations of Christian ideas, the promulgation of which was the true mission of the church. And there is no detour the holy spirit will not make to reach its goal.

Let us corroborate this analysis by examining specific situations with this pattern in mind. The purpose will be well served by an analysis of the conquest of European feudalism by the bourgeoisie.

There has never been a feudal system that had its origins in Christian principles. As I have pointed out previously, the Jews succumbed to only a single monarchic phase that was opposed to the Mosaic intention. The way Jesus selected his Apostles totally disregarded their lineage. Christianity penetrated first the Byzantine and later on the Germanic civilizations. Its clerical hierarchy, only tolerated at first, assumed feudal manners and even feudal positions when Christianity became the state religion and the higher clergy became part of the establishment. As a rule high ecclesiastics did not conduct themselves much better than the secular lords, and at times they behaved even more badly. The members of the clerical hierarchy were very largely recruited from among the aristocracy. In short, a grotesque situation arose.

First of all, the basis of feudalism was unmistakably mythological. The founder of a dynasty claimed descent from the sun god or from Venus. Attempts to provide a rational foundation for hereditary rule by the grace of God are nothing but myths, attempts to rationalize feudal hereditary privileges.

But Christian officialdom let itself be used to offer Christian justification for feudalism. At best, Christianity succeeded in mitigating the social iniquities of feudalism.

The alliance of "throne and altar" seemed an indissoluble union.

The rising bourgeoisie and the exploited peasantry faced the aristocracy. Overt antifeudal movements emerged, which justified themselves in Christian terms. Rejected by the church, however, they were driven into the arms of the heretics. The church could not free itself of its alliance with the feudal system, and thus could not offer shelter to the antifeudal forces. It would have taken the most radical sociological changes to disrupt the symbiosis that had become established between the ecclesiastical hierarchy and the feudal system.

The revolutionary wave of antifeudalism reached its climax in America and in France, where it led to revolution. The American revolution drew its inspiration from dissenting Christian sects. The tenor of the French revolution, on the other hand, was anti-Christian. Liberalism, the ideology of the bourgeoisie, did not triumph widely at that time. But by the middle of the nineteenth century, it had already become clear that liberalism was here to stay. It seems worth pointing out that American liberalism received much less attention than the liberalism that arose in France, even though it is clear by now that American liberalism has been incomparably more influential.

As late as 1832, Pope Gregory XVI in his encyclical Mirari Vos still tried to uphold and buttress the feudalism of secular as well as of spiritual lords. The justification of feudalism given in that encyclical is as feeble as any ever offered.

Leo XIII had seen that bourgeois liberalism had entrenched itself. Until Leo made his attempt to negotiate with the French "republic of freemasons," those Frenchmen were (as the Soviets were to be a century or so later) regarded as Satan's spawn by doctrinaire Christians. Accordingly, all Roman Catholics who championed the ideology of liberalism were regarded as dissenters, as people who had betrayed Christianity to Satan.

Once the church had adapted itself to the new power structure by recognizing liberalism as acceptable in Christian terms, the Christian liberals found themselves rehabilitated. They had become "possible Christians." The spokesmen of the church's natural-law doctrine now began to discern Christian elements even in the republican form of government and in democracy. In addition to anti-Christian liberalism and later on non-Christian liberalism, Christian liberalism came into being and became increasingly important.

It must be admitted, however, that capitalist liberalism was for long treated with frosty reserve, which began to thaw only at the time of the Second Vatican Council, after the United States and its allies had won World War II and become the greatest power on earth. The fact of this aloofness sheds some light on the extreme eagerness with which the church, before that victory, had made common cause with fascism, a secondary feudalism, in its Spanish, Italian, and Austrian variants. Pope Pius XII, for example, had decorated Franco with the Order of Christ. Pius, a typical clerical exponent of secondary feudalism, never developed a positive attitude toward liberal democracy.

But a distinction is in order here, if we are to understand the relationship of today's church with democracy. The de facto recognition of a new social structure signifies only our willingness to tolerate it, and does not necessarily imply that we are its enthusiastic supporters. Still, once the liberal Catholics had been accepted as "possible," and once the natural-law theologians had gradually abandoned feudalism and come to terms with liberalism in the church, a liberal laity could develop. This laity had grown sufficiently large at the decisive moment—in 1945, when the fascist regimes in central Europe were collapsing—to make possible Christian democratic coalitions such as the Christian Democratic Union.

After the allied victory and the postwar emergence of the American nation as the strongest power in the world, the unequivocal recognition of liberal democracy by the church had become inevitable. The church accepted the realities that the principles proclaimed in Mirari Vos had to be abandoned, and that liberal democracy had to be regarded as a possible, and indeed desirable form of government.

The victory of liberal democracy over the secondary feudalism of the fascist regimes is primarily responsible for the fact that Pope John XXIII was able to introduce liberal principles into the church. He granted a large measure of freedom of speech and discussion within the Roman Catholic church, although these freedoms have not yet been crystallized in canon law. This departure triggered new developments in many areas and greatly stimulated the interest that the world takes in the Roman Catholic church.

Freedom of conscience, which has existed in theory ever since Saint Thomas Aquinas defended it, now also exists in practice—to a degree. It is a necessary precondition for the creative working of the holy spirit. To have wrested this freedom from the church, to have won it for the church, is the great achievement especially of the American Christian heretics and of the anti-Christian fighters of the French revolution.

In the early laissez-faire days of capitalism the bourgeoisie soon bared its un-Christian fangs. Another round began. Even before the church had fully accepted liberalism, it became necessary to come to the defense of the proletarian masses.

Socialist utopias had been visualized by Christians for centuries. Individual Christians and progressive clerics had recognized in the early days of rampant capitalism that it was not enough to reform capitalism or cover it over with Christian whitewash. A total restructuring of society was needed. Accordingly, they were developing a concept of revolution.

To prevent misunderstanding, I wish to state quite clearly that every social system has, along with its short-comings, values that deserve to be carried over into the next system. Certain aspects of the feudal order can be adopted quite naturally by a capitalistic or socialist society because they do not require the existence of a servant class. Certain essential human freedoms of liberal democracy—conscience, speech, assembly, for example—must continue to survive in a socialist society. But it is not necessary that the private-enterprise system in its present form survive.

The action of the Catholic hierarchy in taking a stand against Christian socialism caused an anti-Christian socialist labor movement to rise on the continent, a movement of a power and drive incomparably stronger than any of the Christian socialist movements. This anti-Christian labor movement drew support from Christian dissenters. It opposed capitalism as such, and proposed to replace it by a social system altogether new and, in essence, certainly much more Christian. Just as liberalism had prompted the church to become more liberal, so anti-Christian socialism recalled to the church its duty to become truly social.

But the church's interests had become identified with those of the existing state, and this was even more true of the Eastern Orthodox church than of the Roman Catholic church. Sociologically the church was allied with the ruling classes. This fact prompted those who rose to power by revolution to attack the church with special virulence.

Another round in the great contest now began. Leo XIII had given de facto recognition to capitalism. John XXIII, for more profound reasons, now recognized socialism. First of all he understood that the communist regimes could no longer be liquidated. In evaluating their anticlerical virulence he probably took into account how miserably the church had failed in social issues. In his love of all mankind he tried to understand also the enemies of Christianity.

This change entailed a revision of the status of the dissenting Christian groups in the socialist camp. Official natural-law theologians had only barely got as far as capitalism, that is modified, enlightened capitalism. But there already exists a new group of men who by their more progressive ways will provide Catholicism with a support in the socialist order of tomorrow.

Let us look at the situation in predominantly Roman Catholic Austria, a neutral country under western influence. (Though Austria has hardly moved so far to the left as, for example, countries in South America have, I choose it because developments are more accessible to me.) The leading natural-law theologians who represent the official church are perhaps Johannes Messner and René Marcic. These men have got as far as offering a Christian defense for enlightened capitalism.

Johann Kleinhappl and Albert Massiczek, on the other hand, are true progressives. Kleinhappl, a human being decent to the core, was once a Jesuit and professor of moral theology at Innsbruck. Like the much younger Massiczek, he regards the ownership of the means of production as a moral problem. Both men consider it immoral in terms of Christian doctrine that some men own the means of production while others provide the labor. Just as the bourgeoisie discovered the rights of man, so Marxists believe they have discovered the right to the means of production as a new human right.

Collective ownership of the means of production is intended to eradicate wage slavery, and thereby enable man to experience a new moral relation to his work. It is hoped that collective ownership will eliminate the deep alienation and debasement suffered by those who sell their productive energies. Marxism, as it were, thus proclaims its newly discovered natural right, that of man's common possession of the means of production.

To get back to Kleinhappl. In *Katholische Kirche und scholastisches Naturrecht: Zur Frage der Freiheit* (Catholic Church and Scholastic Natural Law: On the Question of Freedom), August M. Knoll wrote:

> An especially daring spirit is Johann Kleinhappl, who began his active career immediately after 1945 as a social revolutionist in Jesuit robes, on the theological faculty of the University of Innsbruck. Three years later, in 1948, he had to leave the Jesuits and his professorial chair and go to work as a simple lay priest in Vienna. Most recently he created a sensation at the 1959 meeting of the Working Committee of Catholic Socialists in Vienna, with the paper "Marxian Social Analysis and Catholic Social Doctrine." He supported Marx as a critic of capitalism and prophet of a classless society and exonerated him for his atheism on the grounds that "Marx's understanding of religion had been determined by the then ruling Christianity, from which no reform of the social order could be expected."

Knoll told me further that in 1948, around the time Kleinhappl lost his professorship and was dismissed from the Jesuit Order, a high-ranking Jesuit of that order called on Knoll to ask him if he thought Kleinhappl should be asked to leave the order. Knoll answered, "No, for heaven's sake, twenty years from now you will be grateful to have such a man." Kleinhappl was nevertheless removed.

But, as Knoll said, the clock of history kept ticking. In 1962, Kleinhappl's book on Christian-Marxist natural law, *Arbeit—Pflicht und Recht* (Work—Duty and Right), was published, with the *imprimi potest* of the archepiscopal ordinarius of Vienna, dated 15 May 1961. By this event, Christian Marxism was officially recognized in Vienna as acceptable within the church. Today it is quite obvious that the Jesuits would be only too glad to have Kleinhappl still at Innsbruck. At the time I wrote these lines, they would not expel him from the order if he were still a Jesuit. It might not be altogether inconceivable today, after Pope Paul's virtual admission of the guilt of the church (his sermon during the Council of Rome on 29 September 1963), that even the Austrian Jesuits would admit that they had committed an injustice, or that they would repair it as far as this would be possible. For Kleinhappl will become increasingly important, and will be the church's alibi tomorrow.

Albert Massiczek, a former member of the SS who joined the resistance after the pogrom-like outburst of antisemitism that erupted in Germany in the fall of 1938 is also a progressive socialist. In an article on the pastoral care of workers ("Standortbestimmung zur Arbeiterseelsorg," in *Der Seelsorger*, 1962), he wrote the following, and we bow to the courage of the editors who published his words:

> The greatest obstacle to pastoral care among the workers is not the workers' attitude but that of the church. It is above all the fact that the church is everywhere taking part in the class struggle from

above instead of approaching the workers as equals.
The average worker has no objections to Christ or to
deeply devout priests or lay people. But he fears the
power of a church, he has thus far observed mainly
to be the ally of power and property. Go to the
workers as a Christian, purely a Christian, wholly
detached from all political and economic positions—
and you will find that their hunger for Christ and
for his church will grow and grow!

Some day the church will be able to point to Massiczek
as an early supporter of its socialist inclinations.

The official social doctrine of the church, by contrast, is
always in step with the times. Marcic, the aforementioned
Austrian Catholic, has ascertained that Rousseau propa-
gated Christian ideas! Marcic was professor of the philoso-
phy of jurisprudence at the University of Salzburg. As an
orthodox Catholic, he advocated the natural-law approach,
which is the official line of the church.

Knoll predicted, in *Katholische Kirche und scholastisches Naturrecht*, that 15 May 1971 would be the occasion of the promulgation of an encyclical called Octogesimo Anno. (He speculated it would be called this in
analogy to the encyclical Quadragesimo Anno of 15 May
1931, which was pronounced on the occasion of the forti-
eth anniversary of the encyclical Rerum Novarum, 15 May
1891.) This Octogesimo Anno, Knoll postulated, by "invoking the 'primary' natural law of scholasticism, according to which the earth is the property of all men, would
for the first time contain essential elements of socialism."

Knoll was mistaken. But only about the timing and the
church precedent cited. The church position that Knoll
prophesied was indeed promulgated—in the encyclical Populorum Progressio, issued on 26 March 1967.

In this encyclical Pope Paul VI proclaimed that it is the
responsibility of the wealthy to use their resources on

behalf of the poor. He suggested that revolution was a reasonable means of achieving "urgent reforms" in some cases.

Paul called upon the principle established by the church fathers that the earth was "first of all the property of all men." Close to the mark as Knoll was, Paul did not refer specifically to the "primary natural law of scholasticism." In fact, Paul cited Saint Ambrose, who said: "The goods with which you practice generosity toward the poor are not your own. You merely give back to the poor what belongs to them. For you have only taken for yourself what has been given for the common use of all. The earth is there for all men, not just for the rich."

In short, the church, as reflected in Populorum Progressio, went much further to the left in 1967 than Knoll predicted the church would go in 1971. Knoll had failed to give sufficient weight to the explosive situation in the underdeveloped countries, a situation pushing toward socialism. Paul had clearly been impressed by the tremendous urgency existing in these countries.

On 15 May 1971 (on the occasion of the eightieth anniversary of the encyclical Rerum Novarum)—Paul VI issued an apostolic letter called Octogesima Adveniens. In this, the alliances of Christian groups with Marxist groups, such as already existed in Chile, Uruguay, Spain, and elsewhere, were by no means disapproved of but—with appropriate reservations—even praised. It would be beyond the scope of this book to show to what extent the Catholic church has already moved to the left, not only by the leaping forward of some of the clergy but also by the official church pronouncements. And this to such an extent that it is now to the left of the Social Democrat parties of western Europe.

A comparison of the encyclicals and the socialist party

programs reveals that the social pronouncements of the
pope in the course of the last one hundred years are reflections of their increasing shift to the left, while the plat-
forms of the Social Democratic parties are increasing
reflections of their increasing shift to the right. They inter-
sect approximately in the time of John XXIII (see Encyclical Mater et Magistra of 15 May 1961).

It might then be informative to discuss now an eastern
country; Poland suggests itself for several reasons.

In Poland there are three Christian political groups that
support the communist regime as well as the economic
and social system of socialism, all of which support Poland's foreign policy toward Germany, but they all desire
to be undisputably Catholic.

First, there is the group Znak. It existed until it was
dissolved at Stalin's death for its refusal to publish a
laudatory obituary in its journals. After October 1956,
Znak's existence was permitted again.

Next, there is Pax, a group that existed throughout the
Stalinist period and opposed the changes of October 1956
(when Gomulka came to power), thus revealing its close
kinship with the Stalinists. Its most important member is
Piasecki, a former Polish fascist.

Finally, there is the Christian-Social Society. It was
founded by Frankowski, a former member of Pax, who
withdrew from that group because of its opposition to
Gomulka. Frankowski had been a left-wing Roman Catholic even before World War II.

Of these three groups, Znak is the most liberal, Pax
closest to hard-core communism, and the Christian-Social
Society somewhere in the middle. Znak clearly is closest
to the Polish cardinal, always standing ready to follow the
cardinal even in political matters and enjoying the cardinal's full approval. In consequence, the members of Znak

believe that they alone have the right to call themselves Catholics. Its position within the state is the weakest of the three groups.

Pius XII's anti-communist decree, which prohibits collaboration with communists on pain of excommunication, was never promulgated in Poland. Therefore it does not, under canon law, apply in that country. Under that decree all members of all three groups would be excommunicated because all three collaborated in the World Peace Council and served on various commissions of the Polish parliament. For a long time they themselves did not know whether or not they were excommunicated.

Cardinal Wyczynski seems to have wanted to let the Polish people know that Znak was the only Catholic group he recognized. He did so by arranging that Cardinal König, when visiting Poland, pay an ostentatious visit to the editorial offices of *Tygonik Powszehny*, Znak's news organ published in Cracow.

Thus the sun of the church's hierarchy shone on the Polish group farthest removed from hard-core communism though by western-European standards it is still relatively orthodox. Since Cardinal König would hardly visit a group whom he regarded as excommunicated, the world received notice by his visit that Znak is within the fold. A cautious silence was maintained, however, on the question of whether members of the other two groups were excommunicated.

Because Znak is in the politically most difficult position, it is easy to understand why it should claim to hold a monopoly on Catholicism. But such an attitude is not tenable in the long run. As time goes by, the approval of the ecclesiastical hierarchy in Poland will gradually be extended to the Christian-Social Society and ultimately to Pax as well, the most orthodox communists, that is to a group that is so much more firmly socialist than is either Kleinhappl or Massiczek of Austria.

Against the clear intentions of Cardinal Wyczynski, who still resists communism, Cardinal Casaroli, during a visit to Poland, gave audiences to Piasecki and Frankowski. He did so on the very eve of his departure, in order, obviously, to escape Cardinal Wyczynski's reprimands. By this action Casaroli made it clear that he was not inclined to regard these two groups as excommunicated, and that he did not subscribe to the statements about Pax that Cardinal Wyczynski had sent to France during the Second Vatican Council.

According to our thesis of the dynamic relationship of church and state then, the Christian variant of socialism is likely to conquer a position for itself of considerable strength even in communist countries. Present conditions in the eastern countries may lend little plausibility to our claim. But it is merely logical that the holy spirit should complete its greatest detour and return to its main direction. Roman Catholic dissenters are particularly important in this context, because they were the ones who kept communications open and accepted the responsibility of living with burdened consciences by maintaining their position in the middle.

In my analysis on defeudalization, which I have explained in my book *Kirche und Zukunft* (The Future of the Church), I have listed the conditions that must be met if bourgeois liberalism is to be realized within the church, this time as a Christian freedom. The church is even now engaged in meeting these conditions one by one, though not without great hesitation.

When I developed those theses, I was fully aware that it was equally possible to outline the conditions that will have to be met for bourgeois liberalism in the church to be replaced by the proletarization of the church, so that the church might be entirely in harmony with Jesus's rule of life. But that goal seemed to me so far in the future that to formulate those conditions seemed a too unrealistic undertaking.

During the Second Vatican Council a few of the bishops, those from Yugoslavia and South and North America, did in fact go so far as to demand that all bishops should practice evangelical poverty. Although the council could obviously not be expected to stand behind these bishops, it remains highly significant that this demand was raised at all. But it is still true that ultimately only a church in the spirit of Saint Francis will carry conviction to the world.

These two analogous examples of transition, one of the transition from feudalism to liberalism, the other of the transition from liberalism to socialism, have been put forth to illustrate that the same phases take place whenever the transition from one social system to another is made. Yet there is one great difference.

This difference springs from the fact that the process that is now underway is being seen in the light of modern sociological and psychological knowledge.

Knoll's prediction that the church would take the position it did take in Populorum Progressio did not arise out of wishful thinking. He saw it as the inevitable result of the sociological laws that he had observed at work in the development of the church. Much the same can be said of Friedrich Heer, who observed that in the days when Pope Leo XIII was endeavoring to come to terms with the French "Masonic republic," pious ladies in Paris were praying to God that this "dangerous" pope might die. (Conservative Roman Catholics called the first French republic the masonic republic because they believed that freemasons had played a decisive role in the revolution.) This observation led Heer to suspect, on the grounds of sociological and historical analogy, that "pious ladies of both sexes" might have been offering novenas for the death of John XXIII when he was trying to establish contacts with the Soviet communists. This much is documented fact: handbills in French and German, printed in Spain, were distributed among the Roman Catholics of Switzerland, urging them to pray for Pope John's conversion!

It may be that sociological analysis of the typical sequence of the phases, which makes us fully conscious of the whole process, is undesirable, because, it forces us to move decidedly and in total awareness, instead of imperceptibly sliding from one position to the next. Because this situation is new, its consequences cannot readily be foreseen.

But that the church will take a turn toward socialism has become inevitable. It will, as mentioned before, be still more clearly expressed in the next encyclical.

Revolution: Its Definitions and Metaphors

REVOLUTION constitutes a subject of greatest importance in our day since a large number of the existing governments claim their descent from revolutionary regimes. We need only recall that the government of the United States of America is revolutionary in origin, just as is that of the Soviet Union. Even Austria's constitution is the result of the revolution at the end of World War I.

As we study the course of revolutions we soon notice certain analogous developments suggesting regularities, perhaps inherent laws. Such patterns may allow us at times to predict the course of revolutionary events in the future. If such prognoses can indeed be made, a science of revolution becomes possible. That would be a matter of the highest political importance even if prognoses can be made only with a degree of probability.

In everyday usage, the word revolution is employed in several senses. In the loosest sense—we speak of a "revolution in ladies' fashions" when hemlines are raised or lowered a few inches—the meaning of the word has become so diluted that it means hardly more than "a striking change." In this sense it is valueless for our purposes.

If "revolution" is defined as the thorough, deep-reaching, violent transformation of a society, the seizure of power by Franco, Mussolini, and Hitler would fall in the same category as the successful establishment of the United States of America against the opposition of the British crown or the French and the Russian revolutions.

157

It seems to me, therefore, that the distinction made by Marxist-Leninist theory deserves study. According to that distinction, the American, French, and Russian revolutions are genuine revolutions, while the takeovers of Franco, Mussolini, and Hitler are counterrevolutions. Briefly, revolution would mean the violent and fundamental transformation of a society in the direction of progress; counterrevolution, the attempt to restore prerevolutionary conditions (though no counterrevolution can ever exactly reinstate previous conditions).

The difficulty with this definition is that the keyword progress implies a value judgment.

If one favors a society whose structure is primarily determined by privileges of birth and in which man is born into his social position, one does not see as progress the transition to a society without such privileges, a society that assigns to each man functions in keeping with his capacity and performance. Seen in such a light, the American and French revolutions would simply be social catastrophes. Counterrevolutions against what had been effected by them would be "restoration of order."

What, then, are the values that may be regarded as progressive, the values that would allow us to make the distinction between revolution and counterrevolution? I propose to regard as progressive the objective of acheiving the brotherhood of man and any means whereby such a goal can begin to be realized. Accordingly, I regard that revolution as genuine that proceeds in the direction of obtaining an increase in rights for the lower classes at the expense of the upper classes of a society. A counterrevolution, by my definition, would be the restoration of legal principles, or at least of a scale of values, that existed prior to revolutionary change.

Thus, if aristocracy rests upon the values of a hierarchy of birth and blood, a movement like National Socialism is counterrevolutionary in wanting to restore such privileges even if it does not attempt to restore hereditary rights to the old aristocratic nobility.

If we accept this view, at least as an operative concept, the revolutions of Moses, Cromwell, the American colonies, the French bourgeoisie, and ultimately also the revolutions in Russia and in China, may be regarded as genuine revolutions rather than counterrevolutions.

Let us also review here the various similes and metaphors used to describe the revolutionary process. Images such as volcanic eruption, earthquake, thunderstorm, explosion, are frequently used when revolution is being discussed. The primary purpose of these metaphors is to supply a conceptual scheme to accommodate certain recurrent features of revolution. It remains to be seen whether they can do more, especially whether they can explain, rather than merely describe, those recurrent features.

Here are the most commonly used metaphors and their authors:

thunderstorm	French and Russian
volcanic eruption	aristocracy
explosion	Lenin
birth	Lenin (pregnancy), Marx (childhood), Khrushchev
fever	Brinton
mythological sequence of generations: Uranus-Cronus-Zeus	Saint Just, Daim

A special position as metaphor of revolutionary energy is held by the biblical image of:

the burning thornbush	Nadeshdin, Lenin

As we turn now to these various metaphors I shall give most attention to those that seem to us most useful.

The thunderstorm, as one of "the most obvious of such metaphors," has certain defects, according to the historian Crane Brinton. In *The Anatomy of Revolution*, he wrote:

> One can outline it readily: at first there are the distant rumblings, the dark clouds, the ominous

160 APPENDIX

> calm before the outbreak, all this corresponding to
> what our textbooks used confidently to list as
> "causes" of the revolution; then comes the sudden
> onset of wind and rain, clearly the beginnings of the
> revolution itself; the fearful climax follows, with the
> full violence of wind, rain, thunder, and lightning,
> even more clearly the Reign of Terror; at last comes
> the gradual subsidence, the brightening skies, sun-
> shine again in the orderly days of the Restoration.
> But all this is too literary and too dramatic for our
> purposes, too close altogether to the metaphor as
> used by prophets and preachers.

Brinton's objections are interesting, although their premises
need to be examined: Are dramatic comparisons indeed to be
rejected merely because they are dramatic? It seems to me that
a thunderstorm may be a suitable metaphor for the external
course of revolution, though it affords no insight into the internal events.

The metaphor of the thunderstorm has this advantage over
Brinton's metaphor of fever: the values it suggests are both
positive and negative, while those of fever are wholly negative.
A thunderstorm may start a conflagration or kill man and beast
—but it is also a release of tensions.

The metaphor of the thunderstorm is related to that of volcanic eruption. Indeed, the two are joined during Moses's
exodus, when a thunderstorm passes over volcanic Mount
Sinai. But a volcanic eruption, despite its impressive display of
the power of elemental forces, seems almost totally negative in
its effects (unless we just happen to call to mind that hardened
lava will some day turn into fertile soil). Volcanic eruption,
like thunderstorm, suggests the early warnings—underground
rumblings, the ground shaking under our feet; the eruption
itself, by which men are buried or put in mortal danger; and
finally the subsiding, leaving behind a landscape greatly
changed, yet not entirely new.

The tremors accompanying a volcanic eruption are an excel-
lent symbol of the changes in a society's value systems that
revolution brings about. The metaphor of the volcano ap-

pealed to Trotsky, for instance, who described a major strike as "a torch thrown from hell." Both the French and the Russian aristocrats of the *ancien régime* knew that they were "dancing on a volcano," that in other words, the old power structure had become unstable, threatened with coming events.

Recalling Lenin's journal *Iskra*, we now understand that he compared revolution to an explosion; the "spark" will cause the explosion of the "powder keg." What was true of "thunderstorm" and "volcano" obviously holds also for explosion, though the simile is less fruitful because it suggests nothing about what precedes the explosion. At best, we might imagine a smoldering wick. But an explosion seems to imply a human agency, an aspect that has often been overlooked.

That Lenin knew something about revolutions is undeniable. Nor can it be denied that he regarded them as something positive. In comparing a revolution with childbirth, he likened them to a process that, though perhaps painful and violent, was fruitful. By Brinton's criteria, the metaphor of childbirth, like his metaphor of fever, has the advantage of being a subject of a science dealing with man (medicine), and thus is more useful to the social scientist than metaphors drawn from meteorology (thunderstorm) or geology (volcano).

A precursor of this metaphor of childbirth can be found in Karl Marx, who notes that capitalism was "pregnant with" socialism.

Khrushchev, in various passages in his speeches, modifies the metaphor by symbolizing the postrevolutionary developments as a child. In his closing speech at the Party Congress of the Soviet Union (October 1961) he said:

> It does not please the imperialists that the socialist countries are growing and developing. They would like to confine us and tell us what is best for us, as if we were children. In fact, the imperialists regard the Soviet power as an illegitimate child. They simply cannot accept the fact that we have grown so much that we are not only capable of learning but that by now we also have a lot to teach to others. Here too, you see, there is a conflict between the old and

the new. Naturally, we cannot and will not live as
the imperialists would want us to live. And so, they
are displeased and threaten to come after us with a
stick. But if they come with a stick, we shall turn
them back with a broom handle.

Again, in a speech at the plenary session of the central
committee of the Soviet Union Communist Party (9 March
1962):

Strange people—it almost looks as though they were
thinking of the Soviet Union as if it were still at
that stage of the first years of Soviet power. But
we have long since outgrown the short pants of boy-
hood. We are wearing man's trousers.

These passages, which are of great interest for the analysis
of the metaphors of revolution—compare the Soviet power
with a child. It is the child of capitalism. But the capitalists
do not acknowledge it; they have rejected it, regarding it as
illegitimate, while the child insists on its legitimacy, that is, on
its right to live. And the capitalists are mistaken further when
they think of the child as still an infant. In fact, it has grown
into a young man who cannot be dictated to, especially not
by a father who denies the young man's legitimacy.

But to return to the metaphor of childbirth. It offers everything that earlier metaphors had to offer. The growing fetus is
the symbol of the situation preceding the revolution proper.

The pangs of labor, analogous to the thunderstorm's distant claps or the earth's tremors before a volcanic eruption,
symbolize the first spasms of revolution. The bloody event
that brings about independence and separation, the outbreak
of the revolution with its accompanying terror, the final severing of the bonds to the old order, and the development of a
new set of norms, are symbolized by the activity of childbirth
itself.

To the revolutionist, the metaphor has the advantage that
it provides him with a justification for the terror phase: every-
one knows that childbirth takes place in blood and pain, and
that, one might say, death stands by the bedside. And yet

childbirth is a natural thing, creative, productive. The pangs, the blood, and the danger of death must be accepted as part of it.

But the metaphor is no longer valid when we begin to think of the mother's care of the infant because the new political structure receives no nurturing care from the old order. Even an illegitimate child, to use Khrushchev's symbol, is raised by some agency if the mother rejects it.

Brinton himself proposed a metaphor drawn from organic life. But his metaphor stems not from normal physiology but rather from the pathological. This fact seems to stress the conservative, not to say reactionary, view of revolution, although Brinton surely had no such intention. He wrote:

> Though it has one very grave defect, the best conceptual scheme for our purposes would seem to be one borrowed from pathology. We shall regard revolutions as a kind of fever. The outlines of our fever chart work out readily enough. In the society during the generation or so before the outbreak of revolution, in the old regime, there will be found signs of the coming disturbance. Rigorously, these signs are not quite symptoms, since when the symptoms are fully enough developed the disease is already present. They are perhaps better described as *prodromal* signs, indications to the very keen diagnostician that a disease is on its way, but not yet sufficiently developed to be the disease. Then comes a time when the full symptoms disclose themselves, and when we can say the fever of revolution has begun. This works up, not regularly but with advances and retreats, to a crisis, frequently accompanied by delirium, the rule of the most violent revolutionists, the Reign of Terror. After the crisis comes a period of convalescence, usually marked by a relapse or two. Finally the fever is over, and the patient is himself again, perhaps in some respects actually strengthened by the experience, immunized at least for a while from a similar attack, but certainly not wholly made over into a new man. The parallel goes through to the end, for societies which undergo the full cycle of revolution are perhaps in some respects the

stronger for it; but they by no means emerge entirely remade.

Brinton, here showing himself a good American, was fully aware of the danger that this metaphor might be interpreted in the sense of an "organic" sociology, perhaps after the manner of Othmar Spann, the nineteenth-century German economist and philosopher. He went on:

> This conceptual scheme may be used without committing its users in any sense to an organic theory of society. The word "society" is used in this study as a convenient way of designating the observed behavior of men in groups, their interactions, and that is all. We find it convenient to apply to certain observed changes in given societies a conceptual scheme borrowed from pathology.

Still, the metaphor of fever has one patent defect: it does suggest a negative view. This fact raises a problem, especially because by my definition only a positive advance can be called an authentic revolution. To a degree Brinton was aware of the difficulty:

> Now nobody wants to have a fever. The very word is full of unpleasant suggestions. Our use of terms borrowed from pathology is likely, at the very least, to arouse in many readers sentiments which bar further understanding. We seem to be damning revolutions by comparing them with a disease. To those of liberal sympathies and hopes we shall seem to be condemning in advance such great efforts of the free human spirit as the French Revolution. To the Marxists our whole inquiry has probably been suspect from the beginning, and our conceptual scheme will appear to them simply the expected bourgeois dishonesty. Yet it seems too bad to offend even the Marxists unnecessarily. Protestations of good intent are probably useless, but we may nonetheless record that consciously at least we are aware of no feelings of dislike for revolutions in general. We do indeed dislike cruelty, whether in revolutions or in stable societies. But the thought

of revolution sets up in us no train of unhappy asso-
ciations. Of more persuasive force with the distrust-
ful is perhaps the fact that, biologically, fever in itself is a good thing rather than a bad thing for the
organism that survives it. To develop the metaphor,
the fever burns up the wicked germs, as the revolution destroys wicked people and harmful and use-
less institutions. On close and fair inspection our
conceptual scheme may even seem to have overtones
of implication too favorable, rather than too un-
favorable, to revolutions in general.

I shall add one further objection to Brinton's own qualifica-
tions and defense. It arises from his comment that the sciences
of organic life are too remote from the social sciences to be the
source of valid metaphors for an understanding of the revolutionary process. The fever metaphor does not lead to a fundamental understanding of the laws by which the course of a
revolution is determined.

When we study revolution in the light of depth psychology,
a metaphor comes to mind that is of the kind that Freud first
used when speaking, for example, of the "oedipus complex"
—a metaphor drawn from mythology.

Such a metaphor, suitable for our purposes, is ready to
hand. It is a mythological image that gained fresh currency
during the French revolution: The revolution, Cronus-like,
devours her own children. This image, superbly expressed in
Goya's painting, has undergone many variations, such as in the
title of Wolfgang Leonhard's book *Die Revolution entläßt
ihre Kinder* (The Revolution Dismisses Her Children). I
would like to extend it further, so that it includes the entire
myth of Cronus, which is of Hittite origin and was later
adopted by the Greeks.

First, a preliminary remark. Psychoanalytic thinking since
Freud has undergone a shift, to put it cautiously, though here
the word revolution would not be out of place. Freud, deeply
rooted in the patriarchal and late feudal value system of the
Austro-Hungarian monarchy, viewed the son's impulse to revolt against his father as a "complex." He took this drive to be

an aspect of the oedipal constellation, although we know of preoedipal, anti-authoritarian aggression.

The young child wants to emulate his father. He wants to possess his mother, who is to him the essence of everything desirable—food, warmth—and he also wants to have all the other attributes of his father including that of being grown-up. Unrealistically seeing the father as the obstacle to the satisfaction of his unbounded desires, he wants his father out of the way and develops a death wish directed against him.

Since the father also symbolizes governmental power, the patricide of revolution is in fact nothing other than the realization of that death wish. Seen in this light, the act of revolution appears to conservative minds as a downright wrong, one that is indeed pathological.

The Swiss psychologist Gustav Hans Graber has countered this Freudian view with a very different theory. According to him, the son's father complex is preceded by the father's son complex, the resentment of the younger against the older, by a resentment of the older against the younger. (This theory is formulated in *Psychologie des Mannes* [Male Psychology].)

At first glance, this theory seems doubtful. What can the small son possibly have that the big father should envy him?

The question can be answered very clearly: in layman's language, the young have youth; on another level, the old envy the developmental potential of the young.

The child is inferior to the adult in every respect but one: its developmental potential. In the course of events, the child grows older and bigger and reaches the level of those who were already adults when he was a child; he may even outgrow them. Simultaneously, the powers of the adults are declining. This inevitable growth pattern gives rise among the old to the fear of being outdistanced by their children, and thereby to attempts at "keeping them little."

Similar emotions and attitudes occur in corresponding social situations. We know of professors who are fearful that their assistants achieve results that throw their own work into the shadow.

The effect of this emotion is that individuals and groups try to keep the lowly low so that they themselves may maintain unthreatened stature. This is what lies behind the rationalizations of the aristocratic classes that peasants must be kept in permanent subjection because they are "stupid by nature," and lack the capacity to become more intelligent. This is also to be seen in similar theories about proletarians, blacks, and other suppressed groups.

The attitude of a father with such a son complex contrasts sharply with that of a good father. Good fathers want their sons to grow and become independent, to develop initiative and character. Such fathers provoke no revolutionary attitudes. But the father with a son complex will certainly provoke the son into reacting with a father complex.

Armed with this insight, we are in a position to understand the conflict in the first mythical generation, that between Uranus and his son Cronus. Uranus rules his sons the Titans with an iron hand until one of them, Cronus, revolts. His revolt against Uranus is understandable in view of Uranus's *ancien régime*. Cronus castrates his father with a diamond scythe, and then kills him. Clearly, Cronus is a true revolutionist.

What is going on under the surface of this tyranny, this suppression, this ominous calm before the outbreak of the political revolution? If we ask ourselves this question, we must be careful not to look for the causes exclusively in the sphere of economics.

We recall that there have always been obstacles inhibiting the upward mobility of people out of the classes in which they were born. Ambitious people who are thwarted in their attempts to rise will turn into agitators and stir up those still lower than themselves. They will develop into leaders of revolution.

It is a commonplace that the leaders of revolutionary movements usually emerge from the upper classes or from among the intellectuals. Beaumarchais, a wealthy merchant who was living quite comfortably under the *ancien régime*, is known as the writer of a brilliant propaganda piece against the feudal system and in support of the bourgeoisie—*The Marriage of Figaro*. It is the basis of Mozart's opera of the same name, the libretto of which had to be cut and revised before the censors would allow the opera to be produced. That revolutionary energy is expressed there, for instance, in the aria of the bourgeois Figaro when he sings that "If our friend, the count, desires a dance" it will be by Figaro's instruction, and danced to the tune that Figaro plays.

More about Figaro later. What is certain is that revolutions are preceded by a stage in which the intellectual elite cannot continue its upward movement. In their desire to improve their status, they revise their alignments and bolt to a new class. Beaumarchais was not satisfied with a good income alone. To hold his loyalties, he would have had to be made one of the titled nobility. But the nobility of the *ancien régime* proved unable to absorb and integrate the upward pressure of those below. British feudal society, still intact though largely stripped of power, continues to absorb the best minds of those groups pressing up from below. The typical *ancien régime*, however, is incapable of doing so.

This process can be variously evaluated. In the interest of peaceful society, it seems to make sense for the most restless elements of the lower, rising strata to be assimilated into the upper strata, in recognition of their qualities. The price required is that of "betraying" the stratum they walk away from. Orwell's *Animal Farm* is a satirical treatment of this matter. When the animal elite, the pigs, are accepted as man's equals, they begin to walk on their hind legs and display genteel manners.

This is precisely the conduct that the Chinese are currently accusing the Russians of: that in order to earn recognition of their state and their society from the "capitalists" and the "imperialists" the Russians have betrayed the "socialist camp." Let us recall Khrushchev's remarks quoted before. The imperialists, he said, could not accept the fact that the Soviet Union was no longer a child but had grown to man's estate and now

insisted on its own way of life. Actually, however, not only the
United States but also France and Great Britain and many
other nations, are doing all they can to demonstrate their
recognition of the Soviet Union's adulthood. And, lo and behold, the Soviets are beginning to exhibit genteel manners.
The illegitimate child now feels that he has become legiti-
mate.

But matters are not quite so simple. The representative of
the lower strata who has been invited to sit at the table with
polite society cannot entirely reject the stratum of his birth.
He has to go on representing it. He does so, but in a tame,
"moderate" manner. His edge is blunted. This is the price of
his acceptance. When a society open to this degree functions
smoothly, a general upward movement does indeed exist, although the rise of the elite among the lower strata is much
more rapid than that of those strata as a whole.

When the upward mobility of the elite is impeded, revolutionary attitudes come to the surface: an ideology of justification of revolutionary changes, a program of agitation among
the lower strata, and a highly sophisticated exploitation of the
contradictions within the society. Beaumarchais, for example,
exploiting the "antagonisms" within the feudal system, urged
the king of France to support the American revolution against
the English crown.

For our purposes, the matter may be interpreted in this
way: Cronus, like all the other Titans, was impeded in his
rise to a position offering more power. Accordingly, he developed a father complex in reaction to his father's son complex.
He represented the elite among the Titans, so to speak.

But to return to Figaro, prototype of the bourgeois intellectual. Brinton has shown brilliantly how unbridgeable class
conflict between aristocracy and bourgeoisie, and the radical
differences between the basic principles of the two classes, find
their expression in *The Marriage of Figaro*. As an example, here
is Figaro's monologue directed toward the count:

> "Because you are a great lord, you think you are a
> great genius! Nobility, fortune, rank: all this makes

a man so proud! But what have you done to deserve
so many good things? You took the trouble to get
born!"

Brinton, however, overlooks one essential, explosive element
in Beaumarchais's *Figaro*—an element that even the Austrian
censors did not notice in the libretto to Mozart's opera although it represents the decisive departure for transferring the
infantile death wishes of oedipal aggression from the realm
of the family into that of society. What we are dealing with
here is the possession of woman, which plays a significant role
in class, caste, and race struggle. In the fight between Figaro
the commoner (in the position of the son) and the noble
count (in the position of the father), it is a woman, Figaro's
betrothed, who is the object of the contest.

In the view of the upper class, *all* women are the property
of the upper class. Women born into it are there to be
married, those born into the lower classes are supplementary
fare that can afterward be left to the men of the lower classes.
The jus primae noctis (the right of the first night) no longer
existed, of course at the time in which Figaro is planning on
marriage. But the count, a reactionary, wants to restore such
aristocratic privilege by subterfuge. How his attempt is foiled
is the central theme of the play.

Figaro, however, is not lusting after the countess. To achieve
his purpose, Beaumarchais very deliberately makes Figaro a far
more decent human being than the count. Historically, however, the women are part of the spoils that go to the victors,
and enjoyment of the ladies of the former ruling caste by the
newly triumphant revolutionists is a historical commonplace. It
is also not uncommon for the intellectual "proletarian" members of the new elite to marry women of the former aristocracy.
In *Report from a Chinese Village,* Jan Myrdal recounts that
in that village the secretary of the communist youth party
married the granddaughter of the former landowner. Another
illustration of this kind of alliance is the fact that a good many
Soviet diplomats are the children of marriages between revolutionists and ladies of the nobility. This is especially indica-

tive when one remembers that diplomacy is traditionally a
profession of the aristocracy.

Let us note one additional psychoanalytic aspect of the relation between the masters of the *ancien régime* and the revolutionists. Brinton noted:

> A final uniformity to be discerned in these first
> stages of our revolutions is perhaps the clearest and
> most important of all. In each revolution there is a
> point, or several points, where constituted authority
> is challenged by the illegal acts of revolutionists. In
> such instances, the routine response of any authority
> is to have recourse to force, police or military. Our
> authorities made such a response, *but in each case
> with a striking lack of success*. Those of the ruling
> class responsible for such responses in all our socie-
> ties proved signally unable to make adequate use of
> force.

Why then do the masters find themselves deterred from
retaliating effectively to the revolutions? What restrains them
from acting decisively? Can it not be that guilt feelings, so
important in controlling the behavior of the individual, are
exercising a force in this social phenomenon.

It seems clear enough that the ruling group is initially not
fully persuaded of the "justice" of its own cause. Only after
the revolutionists have put themselves in the wrong by this or
that excess—and some such thing always happens—does the
old ruling class muster the moral strength for counterrevolutionary action.

In short, the masters admit moral defeat; they are divided
against themselves; whole groups of them may join the revolutionary camp. In this situation, small and poorly trained
bands of armed men can break the armed might of the former
masters. As for counterrevolutionary action after the revolutionists have seized power, the revolutionists can then put in
the field a military force that proves superior to the counterrevolutionists. It also proves superior to interventionist armies,
whenever they participate; they fight half-heartedly in any
event. A good deal of the revolutionists' strength, of course,

lies in the unconventionality of their strategy and tactics as well as in their high morale. Men wholly without military training often turn out to be better strategists than the career soldiers in command of the counterrevolutionary forces. Men such as Trotsky, Stalin, and Mao Tse-tung will serve as examples.

But to return now to the relation between Cronus and his son Zeus. According to the myth, Cronus feared that his sons would treat him just as he himself had treated his own father. This fear caused him to be more tyrannical than a father usually is.

The sequence is very significant. During the final generation of the *ancien régime*, the principles of the new society begin to take their place side by side with the superego of the old, and its guilt feelings, precipitated by the principles of the new society, inhibit the use of force. Because of this the new generation of revolutionists is under the influence of both value systems. At first, the superego that they have incorporated from the *ancien régime* inhibits them: the bolsheviks who seized the Winter Palace in Leningrad released the nobility they had captured on the strength of their word of honor sealed by a handshake. Later, when the defeated nobility took counterrevolutionary action—they did not regard a word of honor given to the "rabble" as binding—terror spread. Now the revolutionists began to kill, much as counterrevolutionists begin to kill only after the—usually unpremeditated—excesses of the revolution. (Two ministers of the provisional government who kept their word were left unharmed!)

Thus the castration of the father, the destruction of his power, is followed by has assassination. In the United States, events took an exceptionally unbloody course, because the defeated British could simply leave the country and return to England. For the French or Russian aristocracy, escape was hardly so easy. The American revolution, in which the old masters disappeared from the new society, bears greater similarities in this respect to the Mosaic revolution than to the French or Russian revolutions.

Once the killing has started, the leaders of the revolution take it for granted that other revolutionists will try to overthrow them. Violent action is now taken against the deviationists to the left or the right. Now there emerges the revolutionary regime of terror. Cronus devours his children.

This emergence of terror constitutes the most compelling argument against revolution. The new regime, in order to maintain and secure its power, seems to require constantly more bloodshed. Foreign intervention and internal sabotage, both of which are very real factors, inspire the new government with a paranoid fear, until it finally sees an enemy in every shadow.

The myth goes on: Cronus compelled his wife to offer every new-born child to him so that he could eat it. But the time came when she felt such great love for a beautiful son of hers that she tricked her husband and gave him a stone wrapped in swaddling clothes instead of the child. He ate the stone, believing it was the child. The mother raised the son secretly, removing him far beyond Cronus's reach.

Who, or what, this woman was is difficult to say. We can think of her as fate, or as the forward-striving spirit. In any case, Cronus the revolutionist was unable to kill all potential opposition in his own camp. Subconsciously, he did not even want to do so. In fact, he must have desired to be overthrown because of his guilt feelings. This is why he did not detect the substitution of the stone while eating it.

The concealed child was Zeus. He launched a secondary revolution, overthrew Cronus's rule, and forced him to regurgitate all his brothers. But Zeus had learned a lesson from his father's behavior. He not only did not kill Cronus, as Cronus had killed his father, but instead gave him a gift worthy of gods: Cronus became lord over the island of the Blessed.

The logic of the myth is truly astounding. There comes a time when it is clear that the killing must come to an end. Robespierre or Beria come to mind. When a point in the killings is reached, the pendulum swings and government without murder begins.

The mythological metaphor for revolution should be applied to entire social strata rather than to individuals. Stalin's partners in crime, with all their guilt feelings, are still ensconced in Soviet society, though many of the traitors and the killers have been removed from positions of influence. Khrushchev himself did not have a clean record, as is well known. But the Russians have realized that it is better to live with such people than to go on killing; and this realization persists. Accordingly, retired politicians of this type are given innocuous functions, such as the direction of a power plant, where they can do little harm. They became lords over some "island of the blessed."

A stable new regime is now set up in which the transfer of power proceeds without violence. Crane Brinton, following the usage of French historians, called this stage "the Thermidorean reaction," because of its analogy to the events after Robespierre's fall on the ninth Thermidor of the Year II.

In closing, I may express the hope that the metaphor of revolution here proposed may prove more useful than the other metaphors I described. It ought to allow us not only to illustrate a much larger number of the facets of a revolutionary event, but also to understand the true significance of such an event. If it does, the writing of this book will have justified itself.

INDEX

Aaron, 37–39, 52–53, 55
  role of, 35–36
Abimelech, 64–65, 66
Abraham, 5–12, 13, 93, 95, 100
  relationship of, to God, 7–8
  sacrifice of, 6, 7–11, 25, 27,
    39, 41, 115
Adler, Alfred, 83
Ahab, 75–78, 99
Ahaziah, 78–80
American revolution, 44–45 46,
    50, 63, 128, 129, 139,
    145, 158, 159, 169, 172
  authority for, 32
  feudalism and, 143
Anatomy of Revolution, The
    (Brinton), 159–60
ancien régime, character of, 1–2,
    167–68, 171–72
Animal Farm (Orwell), 168
Arbeit-Pflicht und Recht
    (Kleinhappl), 149
Aristotle, 127
atheism, and the holy spirit,
    128–29
Augier, Paul (quoted), 82, 132
authority
  human vs. divine, 7, 9–12, 13,
    27–28, 41, 87
  for revolution, 20–21, 31–32
  of revolutionists, 38–39

Beaumarchais, Caron de, 167–
    68, 169, 170
Benedictus of Zacharias, 92–94,
    101–102, 131
Brinton, Crane, 159, 161, 169,
    170, 174
  quoted, 159–60, 163–65, 171
brotherhood. *See* universal
    brotherhood
Bultmann, Rudolf, 35
burning thornbush, the
  as metaphor, 23–24
  symbolism of, 36, 80, 98, 130,
    137, 159

Cardinal Casaroli, 154
Cardinal Wyczynski, 153, 154
caritas, 114
Catholic church. *See* Roman
    Catholic church
Chiang Kai-shek, 21, 46
Chinese revolution, 29, 159
  authority for, 32
Christian church. *See also*
    Roman Catholic church
  dissension in, 125–31, 138–41
  early days of, 119–23
  failure of, in universal
    revolution, 108, 114,
    123–31 passim
  and feudalism, 128, 142–43

175

social structure
  Egyptian, 14–15
  Jewish, 15
Solomon, 70, 74
Solon, 93
Stalin, Joseph, 172, 174
Stekel, Wilhelm, 83
symbolism
  of baptizing with fire, 96
  of bread, 41
  and brotherhood, 114, 115,
    116, 117
  of the burning thornbush, 36,
    80, 98, 130, 137, 159
  of the bull, 51–52
  and freedom, 41
  and the holy spirit, 122

Ten Commandments. *See*
  decalogue
Tiberius, 117–18
transition periods, 143–46, 146–
  54
Trotsky, Leon, 46, 161, 172

universal brotherhood
  principle of, 101, 103, 107–
    108, 112–17
  symbols of, 114, 115, 116, 117
universal revolution, 82–118
  goals of, 100–101, 118, 119
    (see also productivity;
    universal brotherhood)
  and the Jews, 100
  and Mary, 89–90
  and Mosaic revolution, 25, 81
  tactics of, 119–21
  and Zacharias, 93–94

Washington, George, 46
What To Do? (Lenin), 23
Winter, E. K., 134

Zacharias, 91–94, 101–102
  prophecy of, *see* Benedictus
Znak (Poland), 152–53